My Journey To Awakening

Lessons Shared To Amuse, Uplift and Inspire You To Follow Your Life Purpose

By

Michael Sheridan

14508 37th Ave NE, Lake Forest Park, WA, 98155

www.MyJourneyToAwakening.com

Email: michael@dream-analysis.com

Published by: Aisling Dream Interpretation

Editors: Pat Kerr, Katherine Curtis, Marion Coleman
Cover Concept: Julie Sheridan

ISBN 978-0-9557295-1-5

Acknowledgements

Sandy for her support, love and being fabulous!

Paddy McMahon for his insightful books.

Pat Kerr for editing and shaping.

Neal Keyes for all his help.

Dedication

This book is dedicated to Jim & Sarah.

Table of Contents

1. Introduction

My name is Michael Sheridan and I'm 50. I have a radio show in Seattle where I interpret callers' dreams on-air, run educational segments and give detailed interpretations of dreams that listeners email to the show. I run courses on dream interpretation, learning to see spirits, feeling their presence and communicating with them, and learning to see auras.

But this book is not about that. It is about my journey to awakening – the events that woke me up and led me to discover who I am.

Why is My Journey of Interest to You?

We all have a common goal. Life is about waking up. It is a journey of discovery and you've already bought the ticket and are sitting on the train. We each control where our train goes and where it stops along the way. Me? I had pulled the blinds and was sleeping. I didn't even know I was on a train. In my mind, the whole psychic field consisted of idiots, and anyone who willingly interacted with them was a sucker.

We don't all have a road to Damascus event like St. Paul, but in retrospect I guess I had something like it. That event didn't give me answers, but it was the first step in my awakening and it is where I begin my story. It opened my mind enough to begin asking questions. It would ultimately lead me to discover that all around me, life has the answers and that the spirit world is always involved in prompting the questions or providing the answers.

In addition to detailing the events, my story reveals what I learned about the spirit world as I stumbled through my journey. I expect much of my account will resonate with you – hopefully the parts where I was open and not where I was closed!

My intention is to instill within you a desire to reach in and touch your true nature, and to hopefully speed your discovery process by sharing what I've learned.

2. The Spirit World Knocks

I was waiting for sleep to come when I became aware there was something in the room. The hairs on the back of my neck stood up. Tentatively I sat up in the dark and looked around. Not that I could see anything but nonetheless I checked the room. I never expected to see anything. I expected my senses to return to normal followed soon after by my heart rate, but that was not how it played out.

At the end of my bed were three spirits! I'd never seen a spirit before but that's what they were and there was no room for doubt. They looked just like ordinary people – two men and a woman. They started walking towards me and I screamed. My wife, Marnie, woke up alarmed. I began shouting and pointing, "Right there, right there!" She couldn't see them. I couldn't understand why because they were clearly there, and coming closer to me with their arms outstretched! I was terrified. After recovering from her initial shock, Marnie worked on calming me down by getting me to look at her. When I looked back the spirits were gone.

My scientific world was rocked! I had either gone mad, and imagined them, or they were real. The problem was that I knew I had not imagined them. It was early in the night and I hadn't even fallen asleep. They were so real looking. The only thing odd was the way they held their arms at a strange angle. I couldn't get them out of my mind. I knew I had actually seen them and wanted to understand exactly what I had seen. It really bothered me that Marnie had not seen them as it would have been far easier for me if she had.

A few weeks later I saw another spirit. Again I became aware of it shortly after going to bed. I sat up in the room and looked around. This one was different – it was like the torso of a man framed with knotted rope. It didn't have arms or legs. It came towards me stopping just inches away. Then I felt an excruciating pain in my chest, as if I was being tasered. After about thirty seconds the spirit continued moving forward and when it had fully passed through me the pain stopped. Ten days later this same spirit returned and inflicted the same intense pain! I had to do something about it.

Lessons learned: Spirits don't need you to believe in them for them to exist! Don't dismiss or mock people you don't understand. You may need their help someday.

My First Spiritual Reading

I made an appointment for a psychic reading. Until then, I gleefully mocked anyone who professed belief in spirits or believed psychics were authentic, so I told nobody, not even my wife. (Yes, I know I'm the idiot in my own story but if you hang in there, I do get wiser as it unfolds!)

The psychic was Brendan O'Callaghan. I didn't know him and really there was no chance of that. His office was just off a main street in Dublin city center. I made sure nobody on the street recognized me as I knocked on his door. When I entered, he looked at me with an air of recognition and said my father, who had died eleven years before, was in the room. I do look very like my father. Apparently Brendan had run out of blank cassette tapes (wow, this is making me feel old now) and as he was popping out to buy some he passed my father on his way in for my appointment. I was not counting that as a hit. I was still skeptical. Besides, I wasn't there to talk to or hear from my father. We didn't have a great relationship. Nonetheless, Brendan described him accurately, including capturing how I felt about my father. He told the story of Queen Maeve by way of analogy. Pilgrims visiting her grave carry a stone up the mountain and leave it on her tomb. Some do it out of respect but many leave the stone in the hope that it will prevent her from getting out! He said I'm a bit like the latter with my father.

What I wanted to know was why I was seeing spirits, and more specifically, how to stop seeing them. He didn't answer those questions but to be fair I'm not sure I asked them. I was in a kind of shellshock. He did have plenty to tell me, all passed directly from my father. To prove his authenticity my father told me something that I didn't know. He said he used to sit and rub his knees to ease pains in his legs. I was fourteen when he died and had no memory of that so was convinced he didn't do it.

He told me to stop meditating. At the time I was meditating for an hour and a half per day. I wasn't practicing any type of spiritual meditation. I didn't believe in that! I did a form that greatly relieved the stress of my job and I enjoyed the benefits. Brendan was apologetic about why I was being told to stop. He assured me that normally spirit guides do not say what he was being told to say. In summary, he told me that I was a vindictive bastard but that regular meditation had masked that part of my nature. By making me untrue to my nature, I was denying those who came into contact with me the planned karmic interactions. He said it was especially true for my children. I knew I was vindictive, but thought I had rid myself of that trait.

I left quite depressed. I had paid £40 to be insulted for an hour and my main questions were still unanswered. In fact, I had more questions going out than I had going in. I also didn't like the idea that my children picked me so they could experience my vindictiveness. Who would advertise that as a trait on their résumé? Well apparently I did and I got hired because of it!

Later that day, I asked my eldest sister if our father had any problem with his legs. She sat on a chair and demonstrated exactly what Brendan had done, and explained why he did it. Brendan described everything else so accurately I should not have been surprised.

Lesson learned: If the spirit world exists, it knows a lot more about me and my life than I do!

The spirit continued to visit. In desperation I asked my mother if she had a bible I could borrow, or knew an open-minded priest I could talk to. I didn't tell her why, but I inadvertently made her millennium by asking her. I had stopped going to mass years before and she assumed I had now rediscovered my faith. Fr. Bresnan, the open-minded priest, was an interesting man but did not have the answers either.

I Get Help at a Mind, Body, Spirit Exhibition

A few weeks later, I attended a mind, body, and spirit exhibition (my first one) and when I explained my predicament to an exhibitor he told me how to stop the pain. "When you see the spirit, tell it to stop and it will. Then visualize each chakra and imagine a crucifix in front of and behind each one." He said it wouldn't matter that I was not religious as the symbol had enough power for me since I was raised a Catholic.

I had heard about chakras so knew what he was referring to. They are energy points within the body. The first chakra is at the base of the spine and the seventh is at the top of the head. I didn't believe in them, but I also didn't believe in the spirit that was pestering me! I was willing to give it a try.

It wasn't long before the spirit appeared again. I was still afraid, but mentally told it to stop and was surprised that it did. I then did the visualization. The spirit waited until I said, "Okay". It then moved forward, and as was usual, paused in front of me. I braced for the pain he normally brought, but it never arrived! The spirit then began walking through me and I remained pain free. It was a very different experience not wincing in pain. It was quite interesting to see the spirit from a different angle as it passed through me.

Lesson learned: This was a significant turning point for me. I had to accept that chakras were real, and that some psychics are not idiots.

I was no longer afraid of the spirit returning and that allowed me to relax. Now that it no longer hurt me, I felt I might learn something from the experiences. At that time, I didn't know it would never return. In retrospect I realize the spirit had done its job so didn't need to come back. I had started to open up.

Seeing Auras

My interest was aroused, and now that I accepted them, I wanted to understand more about chakras. There were many small spiritual bookshops around town, and I picked up a book by Joseph Ostrom simply entitled, *Auras*.

Auras are the electromagnetic field that permeates and surrounds the human body. Joseph described how he could always see auras, even as a child. My ability to see spirits had 'just happened' so it made sense that Joseph could 'just see' auras. I began practicing to see my aura by dimming the lights, getting into a meditative state, and looking for my aura in a mirror. Within a few weeks I could see it. I didn't see colors like Joseph. Mostly I saw a green or milky white haze around my head and shoulders. I could also see it around my hands and between my fingers. If I discreetly looked for someone else's aura it took a few minutes but I could see it. I noticed it was easier to see in very bright light or even outdoors on a sunny day.

Lesson learned: It is very easy to see auras. You just need to practice.

3. Subtle Guidance

The Puppet Master

When I look back on how I got here, there is one person I must acknowledge and that is my sister-in-law Bernie. She is a puppet master who nudged me on many occasions. Sometimes with soft advice, sometimes with hard. Gently pulling strings that turned me in the direction I needed to be facing. Her skill is such that I remained unaware of her importance in my unfolding awakening for years. My brother Joe, her husband, was also there in the wings but more quietly. Both explored many aspects of the spiritual field, which they frequently filtered through to me.

Bernie had attended many doctors and specialists over a period of years but she was wasting away. No one could diagnose her condition nor treat her. She was a shell of her former self when a relative who saw a feature on TV about Bio-Energy healing, put her in touch with their clinic. Bernie immediately responded to the treatment and regained her health. This was huge as it proved that some alternative therapies work. The impact was so profound that both Bernie and Joe signed up to become Bio-Energy therapists.

This all happened long before I saw the first spirits, and most of it happened under my radar as I was fully engrossed in building my own career. Joe had borrowed the money for the course from me, and a few months later when I found out exactly what he had borrowed it for, I was totally against it. I told him I needed the money back. This put him under a lot of pressure. It wasn't that I thought I was saving him from himself. I was just totally against anything in that field.

Lesson learned: Bernie showed me that my mind was closed to spirituality. When you look closely you will notice people in your life that persistently point you in the direction you need to face.

The Stone Age Guru

Not surprisingly, after I started seeing spirits, I turned to Joe and Bernie and quizzed them on everything they had learned. They were the natural choice as they were in that field. Initially I wasn't upfront about why I was quizzing them, but eventually I came clean. We began babysitting their daughters while they attended Bio-Energy classes and would have riveting conversations when they came to pick them up.

They came back from one class raving about pendulums and a guest speaker they met named Michael Poynder. They also had his book *Pi in the Sky*. At this point in their course they were learning how to diagnose physical conditions by scanning the aura. Michael's field of expertise was Stone Age man, and he showed how Stone Age man diagnosed conditions.

There was no shortage of students in the class who had health problems, and he asked for a volunteer. The student joined him at the front of the class. Holding a pendulum, he touched the student on his spine and silently asked questions of the pendulum as he moved from vertebra to vertebra. From watching how it changed in swing he accurately diagnosed the student's conditions. He did this with another volunteer and again accurately diagnosed his condition. He had the entire class in the palm of his hand. He asked for another volunteer but told him to remain in his seat. He then remotely diagnosed his condition using the pendulum. Everyone bought a book!

Joe and Bernie got a copy of Michael's book for me, and I was greatly influenced by it. It focused heavily on Irish Stone Age structures. It contained detailed descriptions of how they worked with ley lines (typically a long straight line along which earth energy flows) and other energies. That resonated with me. My ability to see spirits removed any doubt about there being a non-physical world. It seemed logical that Stone Age man could also have seen the spirit world, and built the many structures in Ireland for the purpose of interacting with that world. Ireland is littered with Stone Age structures.

Ireland also has a rich tapestry of myths and legends, many of which talk about a time of enlightenment that ended after a battle between light and dark at Moytura in the west of Ireland. The Tuatha Dé Danann were defeated in this battle and are said to have disabled the Stone Age structures so their power could not be misused. We were regaled with these stories in school, and the locations of many of the places were well known and matched with Stone Age sites. Newgrange is a magnificent jewel in the crown of the Irish Stone Age structures, and a chapter was devoted to it in Michael's book. I'd already visited it a number of times and that made the book more interesting.

Newgrange is over 5,200 years old and is aligned with the winter solstice. The fact that it is still standing is remarkable enough! The internal chamber is in permanent darkness, except during the winter solstice. During the solstice, light enters the structure through a skylight above the entrance, and creeps along the passageway to illuminate the chamber. Originally there were two large quartz lozenges in the skylight through which the sun shines. One of these is lost, and the other is in the National Museum.

There is an incline from the entrance to the back of the chamber. This makes the floor at the back level with the skylight. On the solstice, the sun shines through the quartz skylight, and creeps along the ground all the way to the back of the chamber. That part is visible and undisputed. What can't be 'seen' is what the standing stones outside the structure do, and what the structure itself does to the major ley line on which the site is built. The ley line and the polarized sunlight converge at the back of the chamber amid three very large parabola shaped (think satellite dish) stone basins during the winter solstice. So intriguing.

Michael's book explains the purpose of the structure from the perspective of what it does with the energies. It also explains that most Stone Age sites revealed pendulums when excavated, so it follows that Stone Age man used pendulums. Since pendulums are mostly used for dowsing energy, the sites very likely worked with energy. I was happy with that logical conclusion. For the most part, I was very happy with the book. It was very mathematical, my favorite subject, so that meant I could follow the mathematics and understand this for myself. The problem was that I could only partly follow it. I tried it a number of times but it seemed like something was missing or I was overlooking something in the explanation. In the meantime, I practiced using a pendulum and got very good with it.

I was taking baby steps towards opening my mind. My skeptical nature was still very active, but I could accept pendulums worked because Michael Poynder had proven it to a class full of students.

Practicing With A Pendulum

A pendulum can be used to get a simple yes/no answer to a question, or to find a direction. It can be used for lots more, but that's the basic point of it. A pendulum can be any balanced weight on a thread or chain that is flexible enough to allow the weight at the bottom to swing easily and freely. To use it, hold the pendulum thread comfortably and steadily in your hand, acting as if your life depends on the pendulum not moving.

Ask a question that only has a yes or no answer. The pendulum will slowly start to move in a clockwise or anticlockwise direction. Clearly you are the one moving the pendulum, but you are not doing it consciously. By attempting to hold the pendulum steady you are removing your conscious mind from the answer. Something else is then free to influence your movement to yield the answer.

I could use the pendulum for simple yes or no questions. I could also use it to find things, and I played games with that. I got people to hide things while I was out of the room, and I'd walk in with my pendulum and go straight to it. It never failed, and I was as impressed as the person I was demonstrating to. I used the pendulum to check everything I was doing. It frequently took a lot of questions to ask the correct yes/no one, but I figured that the practice was helping my connection and would get quicker over time.

On one occasion I was demonstrating to my brother-in-law Jimmy. He hid an item, and I entered the room to find it. When I was close to it, he asked me to leave the room again. I don't know why I listened to him. I told him it was important to respect how the pendulum worked and not to move the hidden item from where it currently was. When I entered the room again I tracked down the object with the pendulum but it wasn't there. Jimmy admitted he moved it. I tried to find its new location but couldn't. The pendulum never worked for me again! In retrospect I think it happened to me on purpose because I was using it so often. I was not likely to find better ways to communicate with the spirit world if I found a pendulum so reliable. At the time, however, I was not happy. I had lost my best connection but I was already aware of other types of communication and hoped it would be replaced with something better.

The Grand Design

I was working for Siemens Nixdorf and also studying Information Technology at Dublin City University. I loved my work. I headed a nineteen-person team developing a payment gateway for banks. Unfortunately, it required a lot of late hours and weekend work. When I was home, I had studies and assignments to catch up on. I often did these with my new son sitting on my lap. Marnie and I had discussed how doing the IT course would impact us. In the long run it would give us a far better lifestyle, but the short term reality was often worse than expected. Despite me being physically present, it had to be a very lonely time for her. She would sometimes go out with friends while the kids were sleeping and I studied, but we had both effectively lost time with our best friend.

We still had a lot in common, and were passionate about the spiritual books we were reading as we both sought to find answers. That's when it happened. Marnie arrived home from visiting Bernie and called me down from my studies. She put a book, open on a particular section, into my hands. It was *The Grand Design* by Paddy McMahon. As I read, my heart was jumping and I had butterflies in my stomach. It had the answers to my questions.

I did not want to stop reading it, and Marnie had to wrestle the book back from me. For the rest of the day, if she was not reading it, I was! There was a second book published in the series, and we bought it the following day. That way we were no longer wrestling each other, and within a few days we each had read both books.

We had fantastic debates about what we read, and discussed it with anyone who would listen. The books were short but they packed a punch. Other books we had read circled around a kernel of truth, but these just hit the nail on the head with a 'this is how it is' approach.

The books were channeled, which meant the author communicated with a spirit who told him what to write. A few months earlier that would have been ludicrous to me, but now I couldn't get enough of them. They resonated with me, and as I read, it was like I was remembering something I already knew. Our passion convinced a lot of family and friends to also read the books, and everyone felt the same way. They just made sense.

They explained life in the spirit world and why we come to earth in the first place. They introduced me to guides (spirits assigned to help you throughout your life). They talked about earth bound spirits and channeling (communication with spirits). They suggested putting a protection in place, so that spirits who would be detrimental to achieving your life purpose, are blocked from affecting you. I began talking with my guides regularly and asked for that protection. I couldn't hear their answers but I trusted they could hear me.

Lesson learned: I am a spirit, incarnated to learn through experience and thereby increase awareness of who I am. I have a life purpose designed to help me achieve that awareness. I have guides working in the spirit world to ensure I stay on my path. They can help me with anything, as long as I ask for help.

The Red Spirit

After reading Paddy's books, I asked my guides to help me channel, and for the first time in quite a while I was visited by another spirit. It arrived shortly after I got into bed. I never found out why they always visited shortly after I got into bed! Anyway, the room was pitch black. I looked around and saw a small red orb enter the room. It was slightly bigger than a baseball. It moved swiftly over to within a foot of where I was lying, and hovered about five feet off the ground. It then started to elongate and get much brighter. It filled the room with light. I could have comfortably read a book by the light emanating from it. It was probably about 7 feet tall fully elongated, but still very thin. Then I felt two piercing pains in my neck, just below and slightly behind my right ear. Along with the pain came extremely loud sounds. They were like beeps of all different frequencies and sounded like they were being played backwards. I figured this visitation was because I asked for assistance with channeling. The pain grew and felt like something was sawing into my neck. I wasn't afraid this time, but I closed my eyes because of the pain. Eventually I couldn't take it anymore and asked it to stop. It abruptly stopped and left the room.

I turned to Marnie and commented that I just saw a red one. "You know what's red, don't you?" she questioned. I knew she meant the devil so I ignored her remark. This had happened after talking to my guides and putting up protection so I wasn't going to make any connections like that.

My ear throbbed for the rest of the night and I was slightly sorry I didn't let it finish the job. The following day I visited my brother Joe to have him scan my aura. Joe and Bernie had recently completed the Bio-Energy Healing course. Bio-Energy involves scanning the aura for problems and then drawing energy through the body or projecting energy into the body to heal it. I asked him to just scan me and to not do any energy work. I didn't give him any clues. I wanted an independent check to make sure it wasn't in my mind. I already knew it wasn't but this would be outside confirmation. He scanned me for a few seconds and said, "Just below your right ear." I didn't tell him what had happened but I was thrilled.

I spoke to my guides on the way home and told them if they came back to finish the job, I would let them complete it next time.

Within a few days the red spirit returned. Just as before, the small red orb entered the room, quickly elongated and got brighter after it approached me. I felt the piercing pain again. I pushed my head into the pillow and just grimaced through it. In just a few minutes the spirit was done, and was gone. My ear had remained sore since the previous visit but now there was no pain.

I got a strong sense to not get any energy work done for some time. It felt to me like scaffolding had been erected to effect energy pathway changes in my body. I felt like I was in a bubble of pressure. Nothing was unpleasant but it was definitely noticeable. I figured that when that feeling subsided, the work would be done, and I would be able to hear my guides clearly.

About two weeks later, I felt like I was getting the flu, and again walked to my brother's house. He wasn't there but Bernie was. I asked her if Bio-Energy worked on flu-like symptoms. She said it did and worked her magic. Although she never touched me, it felt like she literally had her hands inside my stomach and was swirling the contents around. I was very close to vomiting while she worked on me.

When she was done I felt better. My symptoms were almost gone and my head was clearer. Then, what I had just done dawned on me. I couldn't believe my stupidity. As I walked home I felt like someone had just pricked a large balloon and it was leaking air pressure. I could sense the point in my aura where it was happening and I tried to visualize sealing the leak. It didn't work. For the rest of the day and most of the next, I could feel the pressure releasing. I knew I had screwed up. I asked that the red spirit return to repair anything if needed, but as far as I know, it never came back.

I didn't get the ability to hear my guides.

Lesson learned: Getting what you ask for may involve temporary pain.

The Healing Spirit

It never dawned on me that spirits fell into different classifications until I saw the one in my friend's house in Germany. This was the third type of spirit I saw, the third that I would classify as a spirit that knew it was a spirit and knew it was interacting with the physical world. As I write this I realize that I've never even told my friend about it.

My work with Siemens Nixdorf, Europe's largest software company at the time, required frequent travel to Munich, a truly beautiful place. I had become good friends with my German counterpart, Robert Weigersdorfer. I'd been out to his new house and had met his wife, Sabina, a few times. They invited me to bring my wife with me the next time I visited, and to stay for the weekend, so I did.

True to his nature, Robert threw a great party with several visitors coming to say hello. My German is below basic. I can order food and ask for directions but then not necessarily understand the directions I get. Marnie on the other hand, had no German whatsoever.

At the party Marnie conversed with Robert's aunt, who didn't have a word of English. We thought them an odd pair, given that neither could understand the other, and expected their conversation to last all of two minutes, but they chatted for two hours! On a few occasions Robert and I went to their table to check in on them, and were amazed that despite the fact that neither should have understood the other, they were deep in conversation. Robert called a halt at one point to quiz each about what they thought the other was saying, and sure enough they were right on the money. I still don't understand how they conversed.

After retiring to bed on the first evening, I was awakened by what had become a familiar feeling. I knew there was a spirit in the room. Marnie was lying on her side with her back to the bedroom door, and I was lying on my side facing her. Normally I have to look around the room to find the spirit, but not this time. A spirit was standing over Marnie with her hand in her neck, below the skin. I did my usual and panicked! At the top of my whisper (is that possible?) I shouted, "She's behind you! She's behind you!" I kept shouting it, but not loud enough for anyone outside the room to hear. I didn't want to be an ungracious guest!

What happened next was very intriguing. The spirit looked at me with alarm. Initially it didn't realize I was talking about it, and had continued on. But then realizing my awareness of it, it withdrew to behind an alcove about three feet from the bed. It kept looking at me from its hiding place. My shouting became, "She's over there!! She's over there!" Then as the spirit stared at me, I became very sleepy, and a feeling that everything was okay washed over me. I knew the communication that all was okay was coming from the spirit, and I also knew it was the truth. It was more like a feeling pervaded the room to let me know that everything was okay and there was nothing to fear. My fear indeed lifted, and I stopped looking at the spirit and began to close my eyes.

I hadn't realized that I had succeeded in waking Marnie, but as I lay my head down and my eyes continued to close, I caught a glimpse of her face. Her eyes were as wide as saucers, and she was frozen in fear. I was still super drowsy and mumbled, "It's all okay. We can go back to sleep." Marnie shook me. She told me in no uncertain terms that I was not going back to sleep, but the urge to sleep was so strong. She shook me again. I opened my eyes to see the spirit had returned to beside Marnie and had her hand in her neck again. I was no longer afraid. I knew it was all good – but Marnie didn't!

- Is she gone?
- No.
- Where is she?
- She's behind you.
- What? What's she doing?
- She has her hand in your neck. It's okay. We can sleep.
- No we can't! I can't so you can't.

It was only at that point that Marnie realized I was talking about a spirit but she was still spooked. She later told me that she thought someone from the party was behind her with a knife! I assured her that all was okay as best I could and gave in to my tiredness. The spirit looked at me the whole time. I felt it was her connection that kept reassuring me but I was happy with that.

It was an openness she shared and I knew it was real. I left Marnie in the darkness to her own thoughts.

The following morning, I got the third degree! I apologized for my alarm and showed Marnie where the spirit had her hand, "Right there – right where you have the cyst."

As a teenager Marnie had been in a car accident that she was lucky to survive. She was thrown from the car as it went off the road and rolled over. Among other injuries, she broke her collarbone. At the point of the fracture she developed a large cyst, which she found unsightly. For a man it would be a battle scar to show friends and grandchildren, but not so for Marnie!

Affirmations Work

Unbeknownst to me, Marnie had been doing Louise Hay affirmations to clear the cyst for about five weeks before our visit to Germany. We both thought it interesting that this was the point the spirit was working at and expected it was not a coincidence. It wasn't. That day, Marnie's cyst began to grow. It used to change size periodically. It would grow and then shrink back down, so this was nothing new. However, this time it grew bigger than it ever had before and two days later started shrinking again. The shrinking didn't stop and within a week it was just a small blemish on her skin. Of course Marnie was thrilled. So was I, but I puzzled over that. Firstly, I didn't believe in Louise Hay's affirmations at the time. I thought them ridiculous and too simple. Clearly I was wrong, and once again I discovered something could be true without me having to believe in it first. What puzzled me was how the affirmations worked. Marnie was doing the affirmation – a statement of desire repeated enough so that all doubts are shredded and replaced with belief. That part I got, but how come a spirit was employed to carry out the work? Do spirits see you in trouble and leave you in it until you believe you can help yourself? Then they come along pulling invisible strings in the background? Why couldn't they just help without all that?

Over time I have mellowed on this one. I now believe you attract the healing spirits when you are in alignment with receiving healing. I also believe that free will precludes them from interfering with you, even if it is to heal you, until you expressly request it. Clearly Marnie addressed both issues with the affirmation.

My big take away from the experience in Germany was that it wasn't just our house in Dublin that was haunted. It was no longer the only place I had seen spirits. Also, it was the first time it dawned on me that spirits have different colors. They also have different genders but that was not so important to me. The spirit that healed Marnie was female. It was entirely green. It had a full torso with face, arms and hands and it clearly had a woman's chest. It was green like the green you see in hospitals.

Lesson learned: Affirmations work.

4. Embracing The Journey

A Message During My Driving Test

Our friends were emigrating and we bought their car. I purged the interior of religious ornaments. I also tried to remove a Padre Pio sticker from the inside windshield. When I was done it looked like Wolverine tried to shred it! I just couldn't get it off.

A few days later Marnie and I had back to back driving tests scheduled in the car. Passing the tests would drop the cost of our insurance enormously so it was important to succeed. When the driving test official got into my car, he pointed to what was left of Padre Pio, and asked in shock what had happened. From his face I knew my answer was important and this is the point at which I believe I passed my test. "My wife tried to remove it," I lied, "she's not Catholic." The second part was true.

The tester began telling me about his friend who had met Padre Pio. I thought Padre Pio had died hundreds of years ago so was surprised at that. Apparently Padre Pio told his friend that huge changes were coming that were being orchestrated by the spirit world. The veil between worlds was going to be lifted, and in order to be able to remain on the planet, people needed to increase their vibration. The lifting was to happen within thirty years of a global event. The event would happen before his friend passed on. He claimed it had to be coming soon because his friend was currently in his seventies. I asked if maybe the event had happened already but it had been overlooked. His answer was that it would be an unmistakable event that reverberated around the world.

The tester was so engaging that the test flew by. When we were pulling back into the parking lot he told me not to tell anyone in the office about our conversation because they frown on talking during a test. The good news is that both Marnie and I passed, but she had a more grueling test than me!

I really felt like I was chosen to hear that message, and it only happened because I tried to remove the sticker from my windshield.

Lesson learned: Guides can show off!

I Get Kicked Out of a Peace Circle

Joe and Bernie called to my house raving about an introduction they attended for a spiritual development group. Their excitement was infectious and all four of us planned to go to their paid workshops the following day. Since we all had children, we agreed to go in pairs. Their workshop repeated in the evening so that helped. Marnie would meet Joe and attend the first workshop. She'd come home and relieve me while Joe relieved Bernie. Then Bernie and I would attend the evening one.

I felt like I had drawn the short straw going second when Marnie headed off to the first workshop. I couldn't wait until she arrived back with the juicy details. Thirty minutes later she arrived back! The bus had not come, so she took it as a sign to not bother going.

I was ready in a flash, ran down the road and caught the bus she would have been on if she had just waited five more minutes. I was delighted. A second bus later was followed by a sprint and I met Joe at the event. I explained Marnie's madness, my good luck, and in we went.

I soon realized I was not the lucky one. It was terrible. Joe was having a great time but only because he would have been alone and was now enjoying my torture! I had nearly killed myself running for two buses, sprinting and then paying for this! At one point we were instructed to stand in a large circle with an arm around the shoulder of the person on either side. We were guided to slowly move our gaze from person to person, and imagine a word on the forehead of each person we gazed at. When I got to Joe I saw the word 'PLONKER'. I could see the laughter in his eyes and despite my best efforts I burst out laughing, followed quickly by Joe. The exercise had to be stopped.

I was reprimanded by the gob-smacked host. Joe escaped discipline, claiming he only laughed because I laughed. We all calmed down and assumed our peace circle once more. The instructor guided us again and when I saw 'PLONKER' I burst out laughing even harder. Joe held it together. I got ejected from the room. The hosts assured me that this was the first time they had to ask someone to leave the peace circle. If there was a principal's office, I would have been sent to it!

I remained outside until it ended. Joe came out in hysterics about the struggle I went through to make it to the event. We both felt the same about the experience but thought Marnie and Bernie needed to suffer too. They were already on their way for the evening workshop. Joe and I planned to talk the whole thing up as if it was the answer to everything. We did, but Bernie smelled a rat so we had to come clean. Joe enjoyed telling them about me being ejected and to this day still enjoys telling that story.

Lesson learned: Don't push against closed doors.

First Contact With My Guides

It wasn't a complete loss. One thing I learned from the group was where on my body I was able to feel physical contact from my guides. Each guide connected at a different point. They told me I had seven and four were active in my life now.

I was attending DCU distance learning which involved doing many assignments and lessons at home. Armed with new knowledge, I asked my guides to let me know if a section I was studying was going to appear on the final exam. I asked for a guide to give me a signal if it was. What I soon noticed was that I would get a chill down my back when my guides wanted my attention. That was a funny realization as it was a regular occurrence before this, but I mistook their signal each time and turned up the heating!

Now when I'd get the chill, I'd pay more attention to what I was reading. I began noting in the margins which guide drew attention to each section, based on where I felt the connection. I was going to test their accuracy. I assumed they were telling me what was going to come up on the exams.

I was taking four subjects and the only difficult one was psychology. I loved the lessons but I was afraid that this subject might bring me down. There would be eight questions on the paper and I needed to answer five. I put extra study into the six sections my guides had me mark and went into the exam with fingers crossed. Incredibly all six sections featured. I chose my best five and answered those questions. As I was reading over my paper

I learned with shock that I only had to answer four! Aaarghhh! I could have divided the time on my fifth question across the other four and done better. Still, how could I complain?

Lessons learned: Trust my guides. All of them. Each section they identified came up on the paper. Trust the physical feeling I get when they connect too.

I Start Seeing What Guides Can Do

The Dublin bookshop on Grafton Street became my go-to place for buying spiritual books. It was close enough to where I worked that I could spend twenty minutes there on my lunch break. On one visit I had £20 to buy one of *The Grand Design* books that had just come out. Testing the waters, I asked my guides to give me a sign that it was okay to spend the money on the book as we didn't really have a disposable income at the time.

While browsing for Paddy's book I found *The Book of Q*, an interesting book that explained research performed by both Catholic and Protestant authorities. The goal was to determine the true heritage of the Bible, and thus settle any arguments about which faith was more authentic. The research aimed to identify layers added to the Bible over the centuries by people in positions of power, remove those layers, and get to the core gospel before it was modified. The research had taken decades.

I thought the book would help me with the conflict I felt between what I was beginning to believe, and what I was brought up to believe. The book was pretty badly damaged and I asked the clerk if she had a non-damaged one and also if she had Paddy's book in stock. I could only afford one of the books and was going to let fate decide which I should get, depending on whether they had Paddy's book in stock or not. She went in the back and returned with Paddy's book and informed me that they didn't have another copy of *The Book of Q* but since it was damaged she would mark the price down and give me both for £20. Fate had decided I was getting both books! The experience made me realize that guides can manipulate little things in our lives quite easily. As it turned out, *The Book of Q* was exactly what I needed to overcome the inner conflict I was feeling, and I kept it in my treasured pile for many years.

Lesson learned: Guides can influence others to help you get what you need.

I Learn Bio-Energy

It was ironic that I started the Bio-Energy lessons with such enthusiasm considering how, when I was first introduced to it, I was so vehemently opposed. It really showed how my mind had opened. I was embracing the fact that there are two worlds, the physical world and the spirit world. Most people go about their lives blissfully unaware of the spirit world and how much interaction there is between it and the physical world.

I met Michael Doherty and Tom Griffin through Joe and Bernie at the Mind, Body, and Spirit Festival. This was in the early days of the festival, which was held at the Mansion House in Dublin city – the home of the lord mayor. Michael and Tom were already famous to a degree, as they had appeared on Ireland's equivalent of The Late Show demonstrating Bio-Energy Healing. On their stand they ran a continuous tape of that show. Students from their classes ran the stand and also offered demonstrations of Bio-Energy Healing. Joe and Bernie were among these graduates. Through Joe and Bernie, we were already familiar with Bio-Energy but it was still very intriguing to see the huge interest it garnered from members of the public. It was clear that Bernie was not the only person in Ireland who did not respond to conventional medicine.

Bio-Energy involves manipulation of a person's aura. Without physically touching the client, the practitioner scans their aura to detect anomalies. Sensations alert the practitioner to physical problems in the body. It was especially amusing to watch the faces of clients when the practitioner named their ailment accurately or even when they just told them where the physical symptoms were in their body. After the diagnosis, the practitioner stands behind the client and draws energy through them, starting at the crown chakra and then in a crisscross fashion passing down the body through each chakra. When they reach the base chakra they draw the energy away from the body. During this final point, even though the client could not see the practitioner working behind them, the client swayed backwards. Some even took a few steps backward. This really drew the crowds and had many volunteering for treatment.

Watch Out for Kundalini

A few months into our course, my friend, Stuart, persuaded us to take a day off to attend a talk by a renowned lecturer in the RDS. I knew nothing about her but Stuart's enthusiasm was contagious. Apparently she had a Kundalini awakening. Kundalini was recent news to me. It is an energy coiled at the base of the spine. The Kundalini awakening happens when Kundalini physically rises up a narrow column within the spine. When it reaches the head/crown chakra, it frees the soul within the body and bestows enlightenment. If you're skeptical while reading this, you can relax. I was right there with you. I had never met anyone enlightened and so was very curious. We left our Bio-Energy class shortly after it started, sneaked off to the RDS, and paid to see her. It was definitely a bizarre experience but not for the reason I wanted it to be.

There were probably over a thousand people there and they hung on her every word. But here's the problem. She didn't make any sense, at least not to me. I consider myself pretty clever but this woman had lost all frame of reference with those of us still living on the planet. She was definitely in a state of bliss but I couldn't see how it could not be lonely. Nobody was up there with her. Mind you, everyone, except me, applauded as she described her experience using metaphors that were equally confusing. I guess I wasn't as open as I thought I was.

I was relieved to see that Stuart wasn't enjoying the show either. About an hour and a half into the show, we left and headed back to the Bio-Energy class. Stuart felt a little guilty. The experience had lightened our wallets rather than our souls! I did take one thing away from it though. I determined that it was absolutely pointless to have that experience and live in that space if it meant you could no longer relate to people around you. I later learned that this is one of the problems with having a spontaneous awakening when you're not ready. It's best to be guided by a spiritual guru.

The Importance of Grounding

Joe and Bernie were now practicing Bio-Energy healing along with other graduates. Bio-Energy was still a big thing. Michael and Tom would hire a large venue, advertise in the newspaper, and hundreds of people would show up. Many graduates, including Joe and Bernie, worked on clients at the venues. It was beneficial for everyone. Michael and Tom made money from the events, but essentially used their fame to promote local graduates whose client bookings swelled as a result.

As the weeks passed, with the new graduates working on clients, it soon became clear there was a problem. Some graduates became ill after they worked on several clients. A break from working on others recharged their batteries but they would become ill again once they resumed. Bernie was affected in this way, but Joe was not. He could work from morning until night on client after client and it took nothing out of him. Michael and Tom were the same. It became apparent that the practitioners who were never affected, all had something in common. They had all studied martial arts. Tom and Michael were black belts and Joe had been practicing martial arts for nearly twenty years. It turned out to be no coincidence, and Michael and Tom rectified the problem by the time I enrolled on their course. They added Qigong. Qi (also spelled *chi*) is life energy and is the underlying principle in Chinese medicine and martial arts. Qigong is a system for cultivating and balancing this life energy, particularly for health. It is similar to tai chi in appearance.

The Qigong module of the course was offered by Mark Caldwell. Just like the rest of the course it consisted of a strong educational component, coupled with lots of physical and mental exercises. The exercises opened up the energy pathways in the body, and grounded those who practiced. The result of doing this was that practitioners no longer became ill. Few of us could do the exercises properly until corrected many times by Mark.

He taught us how to focus chi with intention. One exercise, termed the inner smile, drew energy into the body and bathed each organ with it. I began to find that I could feel this energy flow the more I practiced it. Its flow was very slow indeed. It flowed more like treacle than water. Initially I could feel the point at which energy entered my body during the exercise but could not feel it flowing along the entire path, then over time I could feel it further and further along the path.

I Find My Happy Place

To add love to the energy, Mark wanted us to remember a precious moment from our childhood, and use that during our inner smile meditation. He guided us through a meditative-style quest to find this memory. I didn't expect much from it, but was stunned when the memory that was unlocked for me was a car journey with my father. That was my joyful moment – and it truly was. My father was attending The Open University and frequently drove from Dublin to Belfast for lectures and exams. I asked to go with him, and despite it being a school day he agreed. I was probably eleven years old. My memory was from when we were only a mile away from home. We turned a corner when another driver, who had deliberately turned in the wrong lane, tried to cut him off. My father sped up while saying, "I'm not letting that bastard in." He looked at me for approval with an open smile. He was having fun.

That was my moment. The feeling of joy in that moment was so overwhelming that tears streamed down my face. Everyone had their eyes closed so I felt safe. I couldn't believe the power of the memory and especially that my loving moment was with my father. I didn't think I had any good memories with him. For that journey he made me feel like a king. I was in the front seat – a rarity for the youngest child of a large family. He spoke using language I had never heard him use. I had never even heard him swear. He was normally very quiet but he shared his thoughts with me and wanted my input. For that journey he was himself, and while being himself he allowed me to feel like a king.

After the meditation Mark went around to each of us asking what our memory was. I had collected and calmed myself. When he got to me I said, "My memory was me with…," and burst into tears. So much for keeping it together. Mark smiled and moved to the next person. He knew I had achieved the objective.

An Extraordinary Reading

Meanwhile, Joe and Bernie began working from a holistic center called the Complimentary House. Many other practitioners and spiritual readers worked there. They both raved about a reader named Dympna Hughes, so I was keen to try her out. Dympna is a very unassuming woman who immediately puts you at ease with her wide smile and tone. She offered me a chair while she sat in a very low armchair. A candle was lit between us. With what appeared to be the greatest of ease, she began the reading. Dympna makes it clear she is talking to someone else in the room and relaying their messages. She kept calling me "love," a term of endearment that I think is very colloquial in Dublin.

"Your father has a message for your sister Mary. He wants you to tell her that *he is listening*. Will you tell her that, love?" She continued in this vein for the entire reading with very clear messages, including, "Your wife is going to leave you. Oh, and God love you, you're going to take her back. Then she's going to leave you again and you're not supposed to but God love you, you're going to take her back again. Then you will leave her and that will be the end of it. Oh, you're not supposed to take her back. God love you!"

It wasn't all doom and gloom. Dympna told me that spirit was supporting me, and I would find doors open easily, bringing me recognition. She said that others in the field would be jealous of that. "What they don't know," she said, "is that you put in the hard work on your skills in past lives."

Just like my previous readings, my father was the first through and controlled the show from his side. I didn't believe her about Marnie leaving. We argued plenty but there was no sign of that. When I got home I phoned my sister Pat in Belfast. Her given name is Mary but everyone calls her by her middle name. I told her I had been for a reading and passed on dad's message, that he is listening. She was clearly choked up. She was going through a lot of emotional stress and just that morning had looked up in despair and asked, "Dad, are you listening?" It seemed like the next twenty times we met each other she commented on how important the timing of hearing that message was for her.

Lesson learned: The spirit world is aware of everything currently happening in my life, and events that have yet to happen.

Training to Speak Publicly

I got a promotion within Siemens and the department head, Pat, dropped an impromptu presentation on me to see how I'd do. Spoiler alert – I sucked! I knew the design I'd be presenting inside out – it was mine after all. I knew all the people I was presenting to as they were all close colleagues. I was so bad that everyone asked me if I was okay afterwards. Friends feared I might have a heart attack, and were glad for me when it was over!

The only person not fazed was Pat. He enrolled me on a course for public speaking and presenting. Pat was great at finding dynamite courses, but when I went along, I thought I was incurable. I still remember the course vividly. It was just one afternoon and there were hundreds of us there. The presenter, Roko Paskov, introduced himself, checked the microphones, and then simply addressed each fear you could have about public speaking, one at a time, and demonstrated solid techniques to address them. He also demonstrated both before and after with each one. Some we did as a group to prove them to ourselves. He was very open. He shared his stories and fears. With a room of hundreds, I still felt he was talking to me. It was all part of the craft he was teaching us, and he was a master at his craft. He finished to a lengthy standing ovation.

A few years later I was presenting a payments system I designed, to a visiting dignitary from Siemens headquarters in Munich. There was no sale to be made as HQ had already purchased a system before they heard about ours. I had given many presentations since my training and now really enjoyed giving them, but this was Pat's first time to see me in action since then. After the show, Pat asked with bewilderment where I had learned to make such effective presentations. I reminded him that he had paid for my training. Two days later HQ bought our payments system!

Lesson learned: Your guides plan ahead. I didn't know it at the time, but my training and years of presenting were essential preparation for my dream interpretation classes and work on radio and TV.

I See Chakras

The context of when this happened was unrelated to anything spiritual. The company I worked for was running a once-off training course and the powers that be deemed it worth my while to sit in on it. So there I was, sitting in a darkened room with twenty others around a large conference table, looking at the presenter and the acetate slides he placed on the overhead projector – bored out of my mind!

I discovered a makeshift clock. Each slide had a number on the bottom that indicated its position in the set and how many total slides there were. I began watching the clock and willing the speaker to move to the next slide. Mentally willing him on, "Come on! You can do it! You're on slide 16 of 44. Can we have 17 please?"

The speaker floated between the screen at the front of the room and the projector. Invariably when he approached the projector he advanced the clock. Sometimes, while changing the slide, he was asked a question and that stopped the clock. If I had Dr. Evil's set of buttons on the table in front of me, there would have been far fewer questions, and far fewer people still sitting at the table by the time we finished! That's an Austin Powers reference by the way – just in case you know of another Dr. Evil!

During one of these questions the presenter was leaning over the projector with the next slide in his hand. There was nothing on the projector so he was in its spotlight. Clear as day I saw energy pouring from where I knew his heart chakra was! I was stunned. I wasn't even looking for it. Well, the course got very interesting from that point on. I spent the rest of the day looking at the chakras of each speaker.

It truly was a great training course. I thought back to what I had read about chakras and remembered wondering how people knew about them. Now it was obvious. Whoever wrote about them could see them.

From that point on I could see chakras as easily as seeing the aura. I couldn't wait to show others how to see them in my next course. But when I tried, nobody could see them – even when I cupped my hands and ran them down the funnel of the chakra to show exactly where the energy was. All I could hope was that just like it had for me, it would switch on for them at some point in the future.

Lesson learned: The ancient texts written about subjects like chakras were written by people who had the ability to see them. They didn't miraculously divine it, or as I used to think, make it up!

5. Dowsing Newgrange

Through Bernie, I learned that Michael Poynder was teaching a dowsing course in Kildare. I missed the first day but was still keen to attend and headed to where it was being held. Michael wasn't happy that I missed day one, but I was okay with it. I could already use a pendulum. He had a slideshow of Stone Age sites and discussed how they operated and how to dowse them. He also showed how a local man was stealing the stone from one site. Pictures taken from the same angle over a period of two years showed how the site diminished in proportion to how much the house beside it grew in size. It was sad to see something that had lasted thousands of years be destroyed in such a short period of time. Michael was clearly angry about that, and had reported the vandalism to the authorities, along with his pictures, but no action was taken.

During a break, he asked an attendee who was wearing a rose quartz crystal pendant, why she was wearing it. She said it was to help open her heart chakra. He explained that it wasn't doing anything unless it was programmed, and offered to program it for her. He sat down, explaining he was going to go to the causal plane to repurpose the crystal. He held it in his closed palm. I began looking at his aura to see if anything strange would happen and was stunned by what I saw.

He closed his eyes and almost immediately his crown chakra opened up, a pillar of light shot up from it and went up three more chakras. (It could have been four.) I didn't even know we had chakras beyond the seventh! The pillar stayed there while he worked on the crystal. It then moved back down just as fast. He opened his eyes, handed the crystal back to the woman and said, "That will be hot for a few days." It was the most amazing thing I had seen while looking at an aura to date.

I asked him about what I saw and he began explaining it when a male attendee accosted him for saying he had gone to the causal plane. The causal plane is one level beyond the astral plane (where our consciousness can go when we sleep). According to this man, only Sai Baba could do what

Michael had just claimed to have done. Rather than be offended, Michael engaged him in talking about Sai Baba, and explained that Sai Baba had showed him how to do it. I knew Michael was a devotee of Sai Baba and loved to talk about him. He had even dedicated his book to him. I never got the conversation back to what I had seen. I found it interesting that I knew Michael had done it because I saw it happen, yet someone with prejudice, loudly took the focus and probably made a lot of people share in his doubt. It didn't seem to bother Michael. I guess he didn't feel the need to argue, but it did remind me of how I used to be.

After the break we travelled to Newgrange to dowse it. The Office of Public Works (OPW) looks after iconic Irish sites, including Newgrange. Michael was clearly known by the OPW staff and was allowed to narrate our tour rather than us have to listen to the OPW guide. He didn't hold his punches, and was very critical of how the OPW had damaged the site. He placed a special crystal formation on the main curbstone to pull the energy back into alignment within the structure. Outside the structure he had us dowse the direction and flow of the ley line that entered it. He also challenged us to use our pendulums to locate the standing stone that OPW had added to the site. He was not happy that OPW had interfered with a site that had remained intact for over 5,000 years. How could they possibly have determined that the builders were short one standing stone.

The ley line was soon discovered. It flowed into the site from the east and through some standing stones, one of which deflected it into the structure. The offending stone was located in double quick time because it was not on the ley line and not over any other energy points. The offending stone had no effect on our pendulums.

At this point in my 'development' I was beginning to feel energy but it took some meditation beforehand. The energy line feeding Newgrange, however, was a few feet wide and was very easy to detect just by walking through it. It had a different energy in the center that the pendulum could pick up but I couldn't detect that difference. I could only feel the edges of the wider energy. Still I was pleased with that.

Following Newgrange we went to a 'haunted farmhouse.' One of Michael's theories is that spirits get attached to certain energies and find it difficult to move away from them to the subtler energies of the spirit world. Using the crystal formation that he used to activate Newgrange, he was going to free the spirit. Before doing that, however, he wanted us to use our pendulums to pick up what we could. While people were milling around with their pendulums Michael talked with the owners. They had several pictures of friends and family and were in awe of Michael's ability. So were we! He used his pendulum to diagnose their health problems from the pictures. He was batting 100 until they handed him a picture of a woman in her early twenties. He did his usual of going down the spine checking each vertebra but didn't pick up an issue. This was normally okay because they had some healthy subjects in the photographs. When he handed the picture back, the owners said she is paralyzed from the waist down following an accident. Michael was annoyed with himself, "I didn't go all the way down her spine because of her age! That was my mistake. I just assumed you gave me another healthy one." That ended our demonstration.

Michael had already dowsed the energy of the house and placed the crystal spiral where it was needed. The spiral creates a harmonious environment, clearing negative energies for about fifty yards all around it. The clear space is sufficient to temporarily remove the negative energy that weighs the spirit down and traps it where it is. Once cleared, Michael removed the spiral and checked that the spirit was gone. I got the distinct impression he did more than use the spiral, but that lesson was not on our course.

6. The Source of My Awakening

Some years after my awakening, I realized what triggered it. I had been meditating for nearly three hours a day and practicing karate for three hours a week. I was unknowingly doing exactly what would make such an experience happen. The karate contained lots of low horse stances, stretching, and tai chi style movements. These all helped ground me and open up the energy pathways within my body, but the Silva meditation is what really switched it on. My daily and weekly practices were akin to yoga exercises and meditation that are designed to cause this awakening.

The Silva Method

I read Jose Silva's book, *The Silva Method*, when I was twelve. I had heard that we only use ten percent of our brain. I thought it was a scientific fact, and wondered what amazing discoveries lay ahead for entrepreneurs who explored the mind. Then my brother Joe bought Silva's book. It was fortuitous timing, plus there was one important fact about Silva's approach – he didn't mention the spirit world once. It read as facts about the mind, discovered using a scientific approach. I hadn't fully closed my mind to the idea that there was a spirit world but this book fit with my philosophy. Ironically this is also the time I began karate training.

When I was twenty-six, I attended a four-day Silva course in Dublin facilitated by Joe Costello and his wife. I almost decided to not do the course because it was expensive and I had already been practicing it for years from the book. I felt I didn't really need it. Boy was I wrong. The course with Joe blew the book out of the water. For the first time I actually felt the meditative state and it was different from the state I had been reaching thus far.

The course was a veritable Swiss army knife of meditative tools. It taught me how to focus my mind on problem solving, how to project my mind into objects (I wasn't very good at that), and how to remotely determine an individual's health issues and work on fixing them. The course culminated with this last feat and boy did it deliver. I found I was really good at tuning in to determine health issues and then work on fixing them.

I would highly recommend this course to anyone but unfortunately you will need a time machine to attend it. When Jose Silva died the course was radically changed and today it is not what it once was. I can say that with certainty because I did the new format courses too. For a time, Silva instructors were allowed to teach both the older format and the new format, but that freedom was later taken away by Silva headquarters.

I Use Silva On My Broken Ankle

When I was fourteen I used to earn money delivering milk early in the mornings. I'd been doing it for years. On occasion, our regular delivery truck would be in the shop for maintenance and we'd have a loaner for our rounds. One such time, I stepped out of the vehicle before it had come to a complete stop. I was immediately brought to the ground with searing pain and bone crunching. The driver, Brian, came running to my side of the vehicle. He then had to get back into the truck and reverse off my foot. My shoe had somehow come off in the process and my foot was flattened. I used The Silva pain control techniques I'd read about and was very surprised and relieved that they worked. The book had said that the stronger the pain, the easier it is to focus on. That was true.

An ambulance was on the way and I lay on my back trying to relax as much as I could and focus on the pain going away. It didn't go away but as long as I held the meditative state it was more bearable. Brian mistook my focused meditation for me drifting to sleep and kept shining a flashlight in my face to keep me awake. It is funny in retrospect.

I had broken five bones in my ankle and foot. The surgeon was amazing and within two months I was walking on it again – albeit slowly and carefully! Two years later I was still delivering milk and on cold winter mornings I limped on that foot. I tried not to but the pain was sharp. I had tried to use the Silva Method to heal the pain many times, but on cold mornings it always showed up. One morning, we were about ninety minutes into our round and as I limped between two houses a feeling came over me and I slowed my walk. I stood up straight and with a deliberate and slow stride, I imagined that I was going to literally walk away from the pain and leave it behind me. This all happened over just a few steps, maybe seven. I got the idea, corrected my posture to one of a person without a limp and then deliberately and slowly walked as if I had no limp. When I got to the point where I would have winced in pain, I forced myself not to. I still felt the pain but I slowly put full pressure on my foot and forced a normal stride. In my mind I knew that would be the last time I would feel that pain. I continued onto my other foot, and when I came back to my previously injured foot, the pain had gone. I had left it behind. It's funny, it wasn't even remarkable to me. I never told anyone about that. I just knew I could do it and I did.

Lesson learned: Listen to your inner voice that tells you to try new things – even when they seem impossible.

Feeling Energy

I practiced sensing my guides more and more. I would sit in my armchair with my back straight, and use Silva to get into a meditative state. I would tune into my entire body and then ask questions and try to sense subtle changes within, either triggered by my guides or by my state of mind. I soon discovered I could feel my guides' energy as soon as I sat down with the intention of working with them. It felt like a coolness spreading up from the ground. Invariably it reached waist height. Many times I tried to bring the cool feeling further up my body by imagining it moving up my spine as I breathed in, and again as I breathed out.

One night while doing this, I felt a huge column of energy moving up from where I was sitting. It was like a freight train and scared the daylights out of me. I jumped out of the chair and the sensation went away. I had no idea what it was; but it was easily one hundred times more potent than any energy I had felt before.

I determined it must have been alright since I could feel my guides before it happened. I resolved to stay in the flow if it ever happened again. About three weeks later it did. Again I jumped out of the chair. This time I regretted it immediately. It is funny how I could ask and ask for something, and then when it was presented my reaction was still one of fear.

In both instances I was the only one in the house and that added to the spookiness of the events. I later determined I experienced Kundalini energy but I don't know if I stayed in it long enough to have the full experience.

Nonetheless there was a difference in me, but whether it was due to all my meditative practice or due to these Kundalini experiences, I didn't know.

Spiritual Healing

I discovered I could sense another person's aura by moving my hand slowly through it. I could detect where a physical problem was present by a difference in how the aura felt at that point. I also noticed I could feel energy beaming from my palms, and when I'd hold my palm near someone they could feel it too. From talking with my guides, and practicing, I became confident with using this energy and worked on willing victims to see if it had any effect. It did.

I would begin by grounding myself and then placing my hands on my target's shoulders. Within a short while I would feel energy build up in my hands and begin flowing. Sometimes I would also feel energy flowing from the person's body along the outside of my body, under my arms, down the back of my legs and into the ground. My guides highlighted the importance of the grounded connection, and if I couldn't sense that, I wouldn't proceed with the energy work. I suspected that people who become ill when working on others, are missing this energy connection, and the negative energy they syphon off their clients remains in their aura to do damage.

My guides began directing me to move my hands to different parts of the target's body. Usually it was just one location. While working, I would imagine that I was stepping out of my body and letting a spirit stand in my physical space. The more I did that the stronger the energy flowed.

Over time I began sensing what the issue was before I began working on a person. I enjoyed the sessions more and more as it was a great time for me to talk to my guides. I knew spirits were doing the work so it left me free to work on improving my ability to hear them.

7. Stone Age Structures to Be Reactivated

I had wanted to visit the Carrokeel Cairns in the west of Ireland, part of the Moytura battle site, for a long time so I was happy to finally be heading there. It would turn out to be a profound experience but not for any reasons I anticipated.

I knew my friend Stuart had been there recently so I phoned him for tips on directions. He offered to come with me to show the way – quite an offer since it was a 250-mile round trip.

When we were close to the site, Stuart diverted me to the home of someone he had met while he was there a few weeks earlier. He promised it could be interesting. We arrived in Moytura and he introduced me to Pearson Walker Beavis, an English man. My first impression was that the word ominous was invented just for him. However, he turned out to be one of the most fascinating and positive people I ever met.

He welcomed us into his home. Large maps were open on the table. It was clear they were being pored over with rules, pencils, and pendulums. About a dozen stalactite-style tapered crystals of various colors were on his coffee table. They were at least four feet long. The conversation very quickly turned to spiritual topics.

Pearson checked with his guides that it was okay to share with me what he was doing. He received their approval. It was soon clear that Pearson was in constant conversation with his guides. I think talking to them was easier for him than talking to us. Interestingly, he also shared that some of his guides only spoke in rhyme.

He had been living in England and, following the direction of his guides, moved to Moytura to undertake his current mission. Using the maps, they led him to a location where he found the crystals. He showed me the cloth they were wrapped in. Over about seven months, using the maps and pendulums, he was directed to a specific location for each crystal and told where to place it. The crystals on the table were the last few remaining and he was still working on where they needed to be placed.

As he told his story I was thinking of how the Tuatha Dé Danann were said to have disabled the Stone Age structures in Ireland so their power could not be misused. I only had to think it and Pearson answered my thoughts, "The West of Ireland is on top of a gigantic rock formation that acts like an energy capacitor. During male energy ages, the energy is fed into the rocks below to store it. In female energy ages, the energy is released from the rocks and fed into the Stone Age structures. The crystals are the keys to the structures. Without them their power is diminished."

I asked if the crystals he put back had activated any structures yet. He explained that the crystals are vital to making the structures work, but they don't switch the energy on. Something else would do that when the time was right.

"Do you want to see?" he asked. He brought us on a walk through the countryside, over walls and hedges. In twenty minutes we arrived at a valley with what must have been thousands of cairns! I didn't know such a place existed. The cairns looked like small igloos made of stone. They each had a perfect dome with a single square entrance and short passageway leading to the dome. The passageway was only a foot or two long. Their rounded tops could be seen for as far as you could see in the valley. Many were covered by grass, but many were exposed and the tops of a few were broken. Pearson brought us closer to the centerline of the valley. We now had a clearer view and could see a huge standing stone at the bottom of the hill. A stone cross was cemented to the top of it. That really bothered Pearson.

I looked at the cairn we had stopped at. It was different. It had two openings. One pointed back to where we had come from. The other pointed towards the standing stone. The top was missing on this one and I could see that each opening, and the passageway behind it, were uniformly square. I was just thinking that it looked exactly like a microwave energy guide I learned about in college, when Pearson began to speak. My thoughts stopped him in his tracks.

"Nobody knows what this one… Wait… They say you know what this one is for." Wow. I sure got a fast acknowledgement on that. I explained it is an energy guide. The hills that formed the valley were like an amphitheater. The cairns around the hills all pointed to the standing stone at the bottom of the valley. The Amphitheater wasn't perfect though. Looking upwards from the standing stone you could not see a large part of the hill on the left. Cairns built here could not point at the standing stone. The builders solved the problem by building the wave-guide and pointing all the cairns in the hidden section of the hill at it. The second opening in the wave-guide forwarded the collected energy to the standing stone. Remarkable!

I knew from my college physics days that the wavelength of the energy the structures used could be calculated by measuring the width of the cairn aperture. These Stone Age masters were pretty bright.

Pearson walked us back to his house, showing us more structures on the way. He rented his house from a local farmer and had gotten permission from the locals to come and go through their lands. He explained that he was a spiritual healer in England and his guides promised to look after him in Ireland until he got this job finished. He said that shortly after he arrived he had healed a local woman of cancer and it was because of that that he got permission to rent the house he was in. I naïvely expected that word of the healing had set him up but he corrected me. "People in the west of Ireland will not tell anyone if they have been to a healer. They'd be thrown out of the community. But, cattle are expensive and farmers will tell other farmers if you can heal a cow. I make my living healing animals!"

Part of what Pearson subsequently shared disturbed me then and still disturbs me now. He said the world was changing and our current way of life would change too. He said he saw visions in which the U.S.A. was markedly different. He thought that the San Andreas Fault would be the culprit because he saw a different west coast of America. However, he also saw a different New York skyline so assumed the fault line would also run across the country and affect the east coast.

He shared some of what his guides told him of spiritual matters. The world as we know it would change as it transitioned into the Aquarian Age. The earth's vibration would become higher, and souls incarnating on it would increasingly be more and more open to spiritual matters until eventually it would become a requirement for staying incarnated on the earth plane.

I met Pearson in 1992. Many years later, on September 11, 2001, I didn't even think about his prediction of a different New York skyline.

We never made it to Carrowkeel. The drive home was filled with questions and more questions as we pondered what Pearson had said. Truly an eventful day and one I would never forget.

Lessons learned: Meeting Pearson, together with what I witnessed, opened me up to the massive influence the spirit world has on the physical world. It is the spirit world that keeps us ignorant of its existence. Most of what we are heading into has been tried and tested before. The spirit world deliberately diminished power flowing into the earth plane, and knowledge of that power, because it was being misused in the past.

8. First Channeling Group

Reading channeled books was great, but I wanted to be able to hear my guides directly. While there were a lot of channels offering readings, none of them ran courses to teach others how to do it. Lack of courses wasn't going to stop me, so I enthusiastically started an amateur channeling group in my house. The plan was that the first one of us that made a connection would then channel on what the rest of us needed to do, so all of us would ultimately channel. Our group consisted of me, Marnie, my sister Marion, and my friends Stuart, Tina and Gemma.

I had read enough to know the basic protection and connection exercises. The core part was that 'the channel' sits in the hot seat with a person on either side of them sending positive loving energy from their heart chakra to the channel's crown chakra. The aim of this is to prevent rogue spirits from making connections. We were going after guides!

We met once per week and had lots of fun experimenting. The channel always practiced with their eyes closed. We noticed spirits were visible in the aura of some of us when we sat in the hot seat. In these cases, the spirit always had its eyes open. It was kind of spooky but in a good way. The spookiness was enhanced because their eyes always appeared red. For these same people we could sometimes see how their guide looked. It appeared as if the channel got taller or thinner, sprouted a beard, wore a top hat or a robe, got longer or shorter hair, all to match the impression of their guide. All very fascinating and encouraging.

We finally had a breakthrough with Gemma. She connected with a spirit that we all assumed was a guide. However, the spirit was asking questions rather than answering them. We determined that the spirit was lost and explained about guides through Gemma. We told the spirit to ask for its guides to appear and help it. It worked and we had our first feeling of accomplishment.

This scenario happened a lot. We'd attract a lost spirit and help it move to the light. Tina began making connections and it was the same with her. Lost souls seemed to be our target market. At one point Tina connected with a group of seven lost souls who claimed to have their guide with them. We couldn't figure that one out. How could a group with a guide be lost? I wasn't the only one suspicious. We eventually helped them move to the light too.

As I write this I realize how abstract moving to the light sounds but the experience is very dramatic. Each time we moved someone to the light the connected channel experienced part of the bliss that the soul experienced on moving into it. Also, the channel lost the connection with the soul once they moved there. We determined that the restriction was on our side, that we couldn't hold a high enough connection to converse directly with a being in the light. That also explained why we kept connecting with lost souls. They are much closer to our vibration as they haven't moved that far away yet.

One time Tina moved a group on, but one of them didn't make it to the light before the doorway closed – at least that's what the straggler reported back to us. Again, this was new to us, and we were all saddened and clueless as to what to do. Later that night Tina phoned me very excitedly. She said she could hear her guide. She said her guide had been watching our circle and wanted permission to read my mind to get the details about the grand design. I said I was surprised that a guide would not already know it but gave my permission. A few minutes later Tina phoned again and said her guide could not get past a block that I had asked my guides to put in place.

It was true I had asked my guides to protect me from any malevolent spirits. Her 'guide' gave me precise wording that I was to say to my own guides in order to lower the protection and allow her access. I refused to say it. I suspected the spirit that had held back from moving to the light earlier was now claiming to be her guide. This caused a problem. Tina didn't want to offend her guide but I didn't believe it was a guide. Indeed, that turned out to be true. Weeks later the spirit eventually came clean and apologized to Tina, but not before causing her a lot of emotional pain.

The spirit got Tina to stop coming to our group. It claimed she didn't need to because she was the only one channeling a guide. I suspect it feared our group because of the positive energy space we create in it. Negative spirits cannot hang around in that. The spirit then became nasty and claimed to have the power to cause the deaths of her sons. It ranted about that and many other things and Tina couldn't close the connection. The spirit could bug her any time it wanted and enjoyed doing so. I cannot imagine the heartache Tina experienced nor the strength needed to endure it. We were novices armed only with minimal techniques. Tina did eventually clear it but I have witnessed spirits bothering people in a similarly negative fashion.

Our group lasted a while longer. Ultimately it was only Gemma and Tina who managed to channel but neither could get information on the steps others needed to take in order to channel effectively. Still, we all learned a lot from the group.

Lesson learned: When connecting with your guides, if you think you have a negative spirit on the line just ask, "Is anyone who is guiding me in this session misdirecting me or misleading me?" If anyone is, at least one voice will say yes. If using a pendulum, it will either give you a clear 'No' or swing between 'Yes' and 'No'. Then simply ask your guardian angels (not your guides) to move them on. Then ask the question again. Your guardian angels can always move them on. Note: Guardian angels are the guides that remain with you throughout your physical lifetime. Other guides may come and go but these are always by your side.

I Can Tell When Someone Is Channeling

I continued meditating and got better at feeling energy both around me and flowing through my body. Then out of the blue I noticed that if I asked Gemma to channel, my brow chakra buzzed. I tried it a few times and then with others I knew who could channel, and in each case I got a distinct sensation that told me they were channeling. The sensation I got matched the chakra they used to establish their connection.

Lesson learned: If you learn to feel energy within your body, you can notice vibrations active in others. I believe it works along the lines of tuning fork harmony. If you strike a tuning fork, the waves it creates will cause any tuning fork tuned to the same frequency, in its vicinity, to vibrate in harmony with it.

Marnie Hears Her Guides

Marnie had shared a dream with me that mixed two subject matters. The interpretation was about becoming pregnant and about channeling. I couldn't reconcile the two subject matters. Over a few weeks she had more dreams with both subject matters. Still I could not figure out the connection. One morning when I woke up, Marnie was sitting up in bed. "I can hear my guides!" she beamed. Then it dawned on me. "Shit! You're pregnant!" She was.

Lesson learned: If you're learning to channel, getting pregnant can short-circuit the process. Your guides can piggyback on changes triggered in your body by the pregnancy, especially your glandular system.

9. I Discover My Life Purpose

I continued to learn about the spiritual field by reading and doing courses. Then Stuart phoned me excitedly. “I just had an amazing experience. I was regressed to a former life and YOU were there. We were in Mayan times at the height of their civilization and I was using crystals to defeat armies of people.” He knew I was interested in Stone Age structures and the use of crystals. I had to try it. I phoned the therapist, George Rhatigan, to book an appointment, but he suspected I only wanted to do it for fun. He was right. In order to be regressed I had to agree to do it as part of working on myself. We settled on a time and he told me to bring along any recent dreams I had.

The night before my appointment I was out with Marnie and Stuart. The conversation turned to family karma. I did not believe in it and expressed my view. They both lit on me, saying my biggest issues were with my mother and *that* was my family karma. They did not convince me, and I pushed it out of my mind as I went to bed. When I awoke I wrote down the dream I had during the night, and headed off to what I knew was going to be a fantastic experience.

I arrived and was greeted by George. I handed him my dream. He only looked at it for a second and said, “Oh, that’s about family karma!” I was thinking of the arguments the night before and smirked. He caught my smirk and elaborated, “You see where you wrote on the first line, 'I was driving the family car towards my mother’s house.' Do you normally refer to your car as the family car?” “No. Never,” I replied. “Then it is clear – family car is a pun on family karma, and the dream is about family karma with your mother.” I had to give up. Forces greater than me were conspiring to get through my thick skull. I decided to listen.

I Deal With Childhood Issues

My regression was not the fascinating experience in Mayan times I had hoped for. Instead it brought me to a former life with my mother and to my birth in this one. As part of the session I began an eight-week therapy to heal childhood issues. George suggested I attend his upcoming course on dream interpretation, as analyzing my dreams would show my progress with the therapy. Later that day I asked my eldest sister, Marcella, what she remembered about my birth. I told her about the regression and the dream analysis I had received. It impressed her enough that she wanted to enroll in George's course with me. I didn't have the money and so delayed. Eventually I phoned George and asked if I could pay at the end of the course. He agreed to it.

Having missed the first week because of my delay, I knew I had to catch up. I brought along a dream, and halfway through the evening George gave my dream to the group to be analyzed. No one knew it was my dream. The woman he selected to lead the group was amazing. She described my current problems and explained what the dream said to do about them. She even pulled from the dream that I was born by cesarean section.

With my jaw hitting the floor I don't know how the group did not figure out it was my dream! I was hooked. I could not believe how good you could get in a week. Who needs to go to a psychic when your dreams have all the answers? I threw myself hungrily into learning how to analyze my dreams. Over the next few weeks I attended the classes, poured over all my dreams, and when I'd run out, I bugged others to tell me theirs. I had finally found something in the spiritual field that I felt connected with.

On the last night of the course, I told George I was a software engineer and asked if he was interested in a partnership to develop a computer program that would analyze dreams. He immediately agreed to it. I understood why when he later showed me a transcript of a psychic reading he had gotten in the '70s. It told him he would meet a person who would put his dream work onto an electronic device. The PC as we know it today was not invented at the time of his reading!

I Begin Teaching Dream Interpretation

Marnie attended his next course with me, and inadvertently submitted a dream on which I had written my analysis on the back of the page. I was mortified when George asked who analyzed it. When I confessed to it, he told me I should be teaching my own courses. I jokingly accused him of telling everyone that. He said he had only come across two people in twenty years of teaching his classes and that the other person was a woman years before. I told him there was a woman in my first class that was excellent and clearly better than me. He said she was the other person and had come back after ten years to do a refresher. I was dumbfounded by the coincidence as it was her analysis of my dream that got me hooked.

With a lot of encouragement from George, my sisters and Marnie, I agreed to teach classes. I chose the name Aisling for my business. It's the Irish word for dream or vision.

I Discover My Teaching Style

A few days before I was due to teach my first dream interpretation class, I got a reading from Peter McCarron. To this day, I still go by what Peter told me. I had intended to run my classes the way George ran his. George's six-week courses focused on one aspect at a time, such as dreams about the physical body, dreams about spirituality, the meaning of colors in dreams, and so on.

Peter is a trance channel, which means his channeling style is more like Whoopi Goldberg in "Ghost" than anything I had witnessed to date. He reads with his eyes closed and in a very upright posture. He told me not to do the courses the way I was thinking, because that would not work for me. I was to do them without holding anything back, to cover all aspects in the one course. That was a huge relief to me and I adjusted my plans accordingly. I was impressed enough with Peter's reading that I registered for his weekend channeling course. It was a very interesting weekend.

I picked a seat near the front of the class so I could watch Peter's aura, hoping to see something similar to what I saw with Michael Poynder. I wasn't disappointed. After the first break I came back to class early to relax and attune myself to seeing auras. Peter was already sitting at the head of the class with his eyes closed in meditation. Everyone returned to their seats and I watched his aura intently. I expected to see it grow in size or brighten, but instead, just as he opened his eyes to speak, I saw spirits run from the space he was occupying to all the corners of the room. They each held what looked like a corner of a blanket so that as they spread out we were all covered by it. I ducked out of the way in shock reflex but I don't think anyone noticed. It was fascinating to have seen and really got me thinking about how much goes on beyond the physical for our benefit.

After another break, Peter told us that the entire time we were out, a huge Celtic warrior guide stood in the center of the room, and just before we all returned, he drew and extended his sword in a pointing fashion and slowly swiveled and stopped to point at my chair. I asked what it meant but he didn't know. He just wanted to pass it on because the guide had taken the time to make sure he saw him. This guide would be referenced many times in readings from this point forward, but just like Peter's guides that I had witnessed earlier, would be operating mostly below the radar of normal perception.

I Fail at Promotion

I ran a successful course in my sister Sally's house. Success being measured by the fact that I didn't die of panic during the course, and the participants were blown away by the content and the analysis of their dreams.

I had no idea how to market but I figured to make money I needed to spend money. So I scheduled a weekend course, and thinking optimistically, booked a training room in the Royal Marine Hotel in Dun Laoghaire. I also booked a large auditorium for the evening prior, to give a free introduction to the course. I advertised the course and the introduction in *The Irish Times* newspaper. Many people showed up for the introduction, so I was feeling confident that my strategy was sound. However, shortly after starting the introduction, I discovered I had two hecklers in the audience. That's the best way to describe them. They were fans of Sigmund Freud's dream work. Thankfully my approach does not match his, but they were not happy that I wasn't there to talk about Freud. Unfortunately, their lips did not remain as closed as their minds. They simply resorted to disagreeing out loud with almost everything I said. They didn't offer any alternative views – just their disagreement – as if it was vitally important that they got that on record.

That experience taught me that there are idiots in the world, and I was one of them. I either needed to have someone with me who could have dealt with disruptions, or charge a nominal fee to keep hecklers out. Hecklers will generally not spend even the smallest fee to gain admittance to an event, as they don't pay beyond the value of their contribution.

I knew they had killed my evening, but I still got enough registrations to just cover the cost of my room rentals plus newspaper advertising. I also received a request from an *Irish Times* columnist who asked if she could attend for free and do a review afterwards. I was excited about that.

Over the next two days the course went superbly, but the reporter could only attend for three of the sixteen hours. She mostly got the first part of my segment on health, which featured digestion and elimination, and that is what she wrote about in her column. Anyone reading it was given the clear impression that I would tell them their dreams were about the health of their colon. Aaaarghhh!

The newspaper feature wasn't all bad. I did get a good portrait, taken by an *Irish Times* photographer, which I still use today.

Lessons learned: I suck at marketing. Charge a nominal fee to keep hecklers away. Take time to control what a reporter experiences so their report is not skewed.

Don't Go Into Business With Others

I booked a second reading with Dympna. She was chatting with the receptionist when I entered, and all three of us got to talking while waiting for the room to free up for my appointment. She and the receptionist were thinking of opening their own center and asked me if I'd be interested in teaching dream interpretation there. The center would be a joint venture between all three of us. Of course I agreed and was even excited at the prospect.

Then the room became free and she started the reading with, "You're not to go into business with anyone else!" This is a testament to how authentic her readings are, as there is no way she was saying what she wanted me to hear. I was disappointed to hear that, and it took me years to understand why. Years later I would forget her warning and learn this lesson the hard way.

Lesson learned: I need to be clear of the influence of anyone else so that I always push myself, or more accurately let spirit push me, in the direction I need to go.

My First Exhibition

I decided to promote my courses a different way and booked a stand at the RDS Mind, Body, and Spirit Exhibition. My listing in the upcoming exhibition landed me an interview about dream interpretation with Gerry Ryan on national TV. Although used to public speaking at this point, I was so terrified I could hardly remember my own name. I do not know how I got through the interview, but I did. True to form, Gerry gave me a lewd dream for interpretation on the show, but I didn't get drawn into analyzing it. That was in part because I was so nervous I couldn't figure it out!

The television interview got me noticed. My talk at the RDS was packed with hundreds in the room and there was a constant stream of people at my stand. Later in the day I saw Paddy McMahon, author of *The Grand Design* books, on the way back from his lecture. He made a beeline for me and shook my hand. I was in shock. I don't think he could possibly know how much he had helped me in my life. He said he saw me on TV and liked how I came across. He offered to help me in any way he could. As he left for the exit I was still reeling.

At another point, Claire [name changed], the host of a popular psychic radio show on 98FM, was passing my stand. One of her crew came over and asked if I'd like to appear on Claire's show. We exchanged details and she caught back up with Claire.

Lesson learned: Dympna, eh, I mean my guides were right. Doors are already opening without difficulty in TV, newspaper and radio.

My First Radio Interview Goes Well

After two weeks had passed, I phoned 98FM to follow up about appearing on Claire's show. She was on holiday and I ended up talking to Aidan Cooney. He booked me on his show that night for twenty minutes. I was petrified about being on the radio. I'd never done it before, but I knew I needed to get my name out there. Clearly my guides were doing their part and opening the doors. It was my job to show up and talk. I arrived before the show started and Aidan took a few minutes with me. He was a total gentleman. He could see my panic and assured me it would all go well. He told me to take advantage of the fact that people could not see me and to gesture if I was getting into trouble with answering a question, and he would rescue me.

When the show started, Aidan remained true to his word. During the first advert break, he persuaded me to take calls from listeners, and to interpret their dreams live on air. He promised that if a listener got stroppy, he would control that, and if I got stuck with an interpretation, he would talk over me to make it look like he didn't give me time to answer. One man called in livid that I would claim to know what anyone's dream meant. Aidan challenged him to let me interpret his dreams to test me. He gave me two dreams and then stuttered agreement with my analysis. People who did my courses afterwards said his stuttered reaction was what convinced them of my technique. It is ironic that his intended action of discrediting me turned into being my best advertisement.

Instead of the intended twenty minutes, Aidan kept me on the air for two hours. He coached me during each advert break. I couldn't have paid for the training he gave me. I knew I would never have a problem accepting an interview again.

An Unpleasant Radio Interview

About six weeks later, still on a high, I called Claire's team and they scheduled an interview for the show that evening. I was confident of my performance after the show with Aidan. Claire joined me before the show and began telling me what she expected of me on-air. She then launched into telling me how to follow her lead and stay relaxed. I began to say that I'd be comfortable because I'd done it before, but never got to finish my sentence. "Let me finish," she snapped. I looked at her stunned. She chided me angrily for interrupting her and then continued her speech. She finished by again telling me that I need to let people finish what they are saying when they are already talking. I didn't know how to take her. If I didn't know any better I'd say she wanted me to walk out before the show. She never asked me any questions about myself or what I might say. It was such an awkward introduction.

Claire then went into the studio and I was brought in when it was time for me to be on live. Hers was a very popular show, and I was immediately launched into interpreting a caller's dream about her car melting. I analyzed it as meaning she was going through an emotional trauma. The caller explained that she recently found out she was pregnant but didn't know if she wanted to be. Claire asked me if my interpretation was obtained through a psychic connection. I explained how it was a logical interpretation of the symbols. Overall I felt like I was in a hostile environment, but I chalked my feelings up to the earlier chastisement.

When the interview ended, I ran to my car so I could listen to the rest of the show on my drive home. I wanted to see if I had generated interest in my classes. Pretty soon a caller asked where they could get more information on dream interpretation. I expected Claire to give my web address or phone number but instead she gave the name and number of a different analyst. There was that unprofessionalism again, but this time on-air. Now I understood the reason for her aggressive tone before and during the show. She definitely hadn't wanted me there. I was fortunate this was not my first radio experience!

I would discover over time that it is common for people in the spiritual field to be negative towards others in the field. I would witness this particularly when I later ran a spiritual center.

Lessons learned: Don't push against closed doors. Astute readers will notice I didn't fully learn this lesson the last time! I didn't need to get on Claire's show after being on Aidan's. Don't expect a host to be gracious or on your side. Be prepared to deal with others putting you down.

I also realize that if this had been my first interview I would have avoided radio like the plague. Don't let bad experiences put you off.

Since then, I have been interviewed countless times on radio and television. Aidan moved on to TV and for several years I had a regular slot with him and his colleagues on their morning show. At the same time, I had a regular slot back on the radio station he worked for all those years ago. No matter how much experience I have, I still get scared and question my ability before each interview, but once the interview starts and I begin talking about dreams, it always seems to work out.

I Achieve a State of Bliss

Working with George, I had started Cutting The Ties That Bind with my mother. The process focuses on ties that hold you back but also incorporates the positive influence the same parent had on you too. By the end of the process, which typically takes six weeks, you are no longer affected negatively by that parent.

George had warned that some people get physical symptoms and not to worry about them. Well I forgot his warning, and while travelling to work on the bus, I felt a pain in my chest. It was excruciating. The bus was at a stop when it happened. I was clutching my chest and looking out the window wondering if I could make it off the bus to the sidewalk. I thought I'd rather have a heart attack where medics could get to me. I struggled down the stairs and off the bus. The air felt good and the pain stopped. I didn't know what to do. I had gotten off about five stops before my intended destination so I walked the rest of the way to work – slowly at first in case the pain returned, but it didn't.

That weekend I had a scheduled follow-up with George. He asked how the process was going and if I had any sensations, especially in my chest. I told him about my experience. I had completely forgotten about his warning. He assured me that what I felt was my heart chakra opening and that it was a great sign. I was relieved but slightly doubtful.

About four weeks into the process I was awakened in the middle of the night. I sat up to check in with my guides. Immediately I was in a state like hypnotic regression, but stronger. I was co-experiencing an event with my mother. She was pregnant with me. The visuals I saw and the feelings I felt were hers. She was digging a potato patch (Uh! How Irish is that?) in her garden with the sole aim of inducing a miscarriage. She was so incredibly sad and felt her world was coming to an end. She had eight children already and didn't want another. She thought she was in menopause and felt the world had gone against her when she discovered she was pregnant with me. She felt she fully deserved freedom from having another child.

I had been told the story of my mother digging the potato patch to try losing me. In fact, it was my mother who told me the story, but she always told it with a laugh so I didn't know how real it was. After my vision I completely understood her. I witnessed the vision from her point of view. She had two miscarriages previously so thought she knew what she was doing. Instead, she was rushed to the hospital and remained bedridden for two months until I was born by cesarean section at seven months. Nobody expected me to live and I received the last rites as soon as I was born.

The vision was key to me realizing the impact of her actions on me. I continued the daily ritual to the end and went to George to be guided through the completion process.

Even before I finished, a transformation had happened. I completely lost my vindictiveness, and was profoundly patient and calm. The latter came about because I felt a compassion for everyone. I found it most interesting that I was no longer meditating and yet I was more aligned with the states that I aimed for when I did meditate. My ability to see auras increased phenomenally. I could now see detailed flows in them. I also didn't have to work at seeing them. They were just instantly there if I wanted to look. I felt like I was part of the planet. If I looked at a stranger across the street I knew things about them. I mostly knew their traits and issues. As I looked at them I would see a friend of mine in their face and I just intuitively knew the traits they had in common.

I stayed in this blissful state for five months. I was permanently aware of the spiritual significance of my life. I felt things in a stronger way. I 'got' how others felt. It was almost empathic. This stronger connection with others was accompanied by an understanding that they were where they needed to be. It was completely okay if someone was angry with me. Their anger didn't affect me other than having to acknowledge it.

Depending on your philosophy you may be familiar with this state as the Dharmic path or living in a state of grace. Near the end, I felt it slipping away. I suspected at the time that I had accelerated my exit from the Dharmic path by being worried about not staying on it.

Lesson learned: It's not okay just to see what you suffered as a child through your adult eyes. You must connect with the feeling you experienced as that child in order to express it and let it go. It's all about the feeling.

I Show People How to See Auras

I had run several dream interpretation courses by now and my favorite aspect of them was always the spiritual dimension of dreams. This allowed me to talk about guides, spiritual gifts, and life purpose. Having gone from skeptical to open, I was eager to share these wonders with others. However, I wasn't always getting enthusiasm from my audience. Almost everyone had heard about guardian angels. Some believed in them and some wanted evidence of them. Some didn't believe in any spirits.

Picture this. I'm sitting at the top of a class, looking at my audience and their guides standing behind them. I'm telling them about their guides but they don't know if it's true. They usually give me the benefit of the doubt because of my analysis of their dreams, but I want them to see it as clearly as I do. Then it dawned on me.

I got everyone to stand up and had a volunteer stand against the wall. I then told the group how to see her aura and pointed to where it was easiest to see. Within five minutes everyone saw it. I swapped volunteers and did the same. I then stood in the volunteer's place and when they could see my aura I pointed to where my guides were. Everyone saw them. I did the same with another volunteer. When we sat back down to resume the lesson everyone was a believer!

I added showing how to see auras and guides to my dream interpretation course.

Newspaper Interview

Newspaper interviews continued along with interviews in magazines. I enjoyed each one but still failed to leverage the opportunities they presented. One in particular was with *The Evening Herald.*

The interviewer was Vicky Jocher. During the interview I prompted her for dreams, to show her how analysis worked. For the longest time she resisted, saying she wanted to keep the interview professional. Eventually she gave in and shared a dream. She cried during the analysis and again said she had wanted to keep the interview professional. I knew I'd hit the mark on her dream so expected a good interview.

Two days later I read a full-page glowing review in her paper. She even mentioned that I had analyzed some of her dreams. Within a few hours of the newspaper coming out I got two calls. One was from an old boss in the Bank of Ireland. He wanted the number of the photographer. He said he needed a new photograph and since this photographer was able to work miracles with my ugly face, he knew he'd work for him too. We had a good laugh and he congratulated me on the interview.

Turning Down The Late Show

The second phone call was from "The Late Late Show". (Not the American one!) This is the same show that made the Bio-Energy people famous! They wanted me to be a guest on the show with Pat Kenny that Friday. I panicked and said no. They asked me to think about it and said they would call back. They did and I was still afraid to go on national TV. I was remembering when I was previously on TV and how I was so nervous I couldn't have spelled my name if asked. This show was in the major leagues. Everyone watched "The Late Late Show", including my mother! I turned it down.

I still regret doing that. I imagine it would have turned my life in a completely different direction.

Lesson learned: Never turn an offer down on the spot. Accept it and then evaluate and prepare for it. Turn it down later if needed.

10. Hearing Guides Pays Dividends

My Guides Help Me Change Jobs

In 1997 I quit Siemens and moved to Bank of Ireland. With a growing family I needed to boost my income. I had developed a payments system that Bank of Ireland used. As a consequence, I had built a great relationship with Dave, a person of influence within the bank. I dropped a hint that I could be persuaded to move and he was eager. Not wanting to upset Siemens, he set up an interview through the normal channels. During the interview I was offered less money than I was currently on. I turned it down. Dave was not happy with my interviewer.

Six months later Marnie phoned me at work with a message she had just channeled. “Quick. You have less than thirty minutes. Phone Dave and tell him you are interested in moving jobs again. It’s important for more than one reason but I don’t know what they are.”

I did as I was told and the following day I met Dave for coffee in an off-street café. He apologized for the offer I had been made at the previous interview and told me that this time I could name my price and when I wanted to start – no interview needed. He’d see to the rest. I named my price and set a start date of five months later. I had years of annual leave built up that I needed to use.

A week later, the importance of the timing became clear. My boss at Siemens had decided that Dave was not appreciating the value Siemens brought to him. To help him see that value, he began limiting Dave’s access to me. I was unaware of that. When Marnie phoned me with the channeled message, my boss had just refused a short notice request for me to attend a strategic meeting in Bank of Ireland. I was also unaware of that.

My boss’s intention was for Bank of Ireland to see the value Siemens brought to them. The result was that my value increased! I gave five months' notice to Siemens and I worked a three-day week for those five months to use up my accumulated annual leave.

I began to worry when just days before my notice was up, I still had not received an offer from Bank of Ireland. All I was going on was the meeting with Dave in the café. On my last day I was very much relieved to arrive home to the offer letter. I became the relationship manager for the same flagship payment systems I had developed. The job was a lot less pressure than I had been used to, and the pay was double.

Lesson learned: Guides are aware of everything happening in your life *and* the lives of those around you. At the time I suspected, but now I know they orchestrate some of those things. They will also use ready access to channels of communication with you.

I'm Warned About a Friend's Health

My intuition had improved but it wasn't something I could control. When it worked it was spontaneous. I would just get a download about someone or something but wouldn't have asked about it. I really wanted to turn it on at will but that would take several more years.

On one occasion, I had just cycled home from work and was pulling into the driveway when I got a download. My wife's sister was visiting us with her friend Margaret. My download told me that Margaret had cancer in her left breast and that it was advanced. Here's the thing. What do you do with that information? I wasn't going to just walk in and tell Margaret that. I didn't have that strength. It really bothered me, and for the next two days it was all I could think about. I mulled over ways to bring it up in conversation. As it turned out, I didn't have to.

Something came up and my wife asked me to take Margaret to our local doctor. Margaret still hadn't said anything to anyone and this was perceived to be a run of the mill doctor visit. However, Margaret came out of the doctor's office with a referral for immediate admittance at St. Vincent's Hospital. We drove straight there. She got x-rays and met with consultants. A mastectomy was scheduled for six days later. As we drove home the conversation was a lot more honest between both of us.

Margaret asked me to do spiritual healing on her, so once a day I spent forty-five minutes working on her. Each time we worked, while my hands were on the surface of her body, it felt like another pair of hands was inside her body under her skin. Her skin rippled and moved under my hands. We frequently commented on this and both took it as encouraging. Indeed, on her final checkup before the operation, the consultant reported that the tumor had decreased in size.

Margaret spent three days in the hospital after the operation. The doctors were happy she didn't need a follow-up operation, and she was happy they didn't remove as much of her breast as she feared. With the operation performed in Ireland, the cost of her treatment was €20 per day spent in hospital, so totaled €60. While she was being discharged the doctor asked where to send her bill. I gave address details and explained about her just visiting from the U.S.A. He said he couldn't promise it but would try to get the €60 waived. He must have, because we never received a bill.

Lesson learned: Trust your intuition when it comes to other people's health. Trust that spiritual healing works.

Regular TV Appearances

I got a call from a producer of Ireland AM asking if I would come on the show to talk about dream interpretation. At the time, this was the only live national morning show in Ireland, so it was, and still is, a great spot. I dressed in my best suit and went along. I was nervous but hid it as best I could. Aidan Cooney had moved from 98FM radio and was an anchor on the show. He asked if I remembered his interview all those years ago. If only he knew how much he helped me!

I was interviewed by Mark Cagney on-air and dodged his bullets – uh, I mean answered his questions, as best I could. Overall I was very happy with my performance.

The producer who invited me booked an appointment with me to interpret some of her dreams. I impressed her enough to get invited back on-air to interpret callers' dreams live. This was a different kettle of fish. On TV, people would see panic on my face, so I had to remain composed while working out what the dreams meant. When I arrived for my second appearance, Mark approached with one of his dreams. When I interpreted it he shook his head in bewilderment muttering that I couldn't have known that.

The crew was very easy to work with. They engaged warmly with guests during advert breaks. They asked how they could make it easier for me to interpret the dreams, and modified their format to suit. It was the start of many years appearing on TV3 with roughly six-week intervals between appearances. Even when I moved away from Dublin, I would accept their invitations and drive there for the short appearance.

One time I had the flu but was already scheduled to appear. I felt like death warmed up. I had it so stuck in my head that I couldn't turn down a request that I still went on. The makeup artist had a hard time making my skin look flesh tone that day. When the camera was on me, I got asked a question that required explaining about the aura and how to clear it. Rather than answer, I told the caller to go to my website and look up a particular page. In my hazy state I thought I'd get cancelled if I talked about 'invisible' things such as the aura and how to protect it. When I got home I was bedridden for two weeks. I never got invited back. I assume it was because I didn't answer the question.

Lesson learned: Bow out of an appointment if you become ill. If you get asked a question to which you know the answer, and the host wants you to answer it, then do it.

Regular Radio Appearances

I was fortunate to be a regular guest on two radio stations on consecutive weeks. On Monday one week I was a guest on Lindsey Dolan's show on Country Mix, and Thursday the following week I was a guest on The Inbox on 98FM. Both shows were talk shows with quick-fire questions and calls about dreams. I probably did a dozen dreams on each show and stayed with both shows for several years.

The Inbox stopped airing when Alison O'Reilly, one of the two hosts, left to pursue work in journalism and TV. I left the Country Mix show when my employment changed and I could no longer organize my time around it.

I never figured out how to make money from appearing on the shows, but it gave me years of practice interpreting dreams live and attempting to be entertaining while doing it.

I Clear More Childhood Issues

Sometimes in life you meet the right person for the wrong reasons. Marnie and I were having trouble and Bernie recommended seeing a counselor by the name of Neal Keyes. Neal met us together initially and then we were to meet him independently for a while. Within a few weeks Marnie stopped going but I continued. Neal suggested I do a program with him designed to clear childhood issues.

The program was based on the twelve steps for Alcoholics Anonymous. Each week we met and did a step. I had homework for each step, which Neal read through and then determined a course of action. I spent many weeks on one step and began to wonder if the course would last forever. Little did I know that Neal only spent extra time on that because I needed it.

By the end of the program I was a changed man, and people noticed that in me. I was so thankful to have found Neal and wanted to do more work, but he wouldn't let me. He warned that people can become addicted to counseling.

Based on the changes in me, my sister signed up to do Neal's course, and she had a similarly profound experience. Two friends also did his course, again with amazing results.

I started sending people to Neal based on what was revealed in their dreams. In all cases he was stellar, but I only found that out because the people I sent reported back to me. In all the years I sent people to him, Neal never even acknowledged that a client I sent had even showed up. He had a code of honor and that endeared people to him.

Today I am still lucky to count Neal among my friends.

Lesson learned: Counseling, when done properly, can work miracles. Don't assume that all your childhood issues are cleared because you worked on them once. It may require more than one attempt.

Marnie and I Separate

In 2001 Marnie and I separated. It had been coming for a while and in the end it happened exactly as Dympna predicted many years before. Knowing that prediction, I didn't want to get back together when Marnie left me the first time, but I was still in love. I relented when her brother and his wife came to visit from America. Six months later she left again, and this time I resolved to be strong. A year later she was misdiagnosed with ovarian cancer and she moved back in. Fortunately, the operation she required was a success and she fully recovered, but our relationship didn't.

The final part of Dympna's prediction came true when I asked for a separation. The sequence of events caused me to question how much free will we have. How could my guides predict so clearly how it would unfold, and how come, even with me resisting, it still happened as they said?

Lesson learned: I learned again that my guides know me better than I know myself. I had free will throughout. I remember my inability to heed advice when I counsel others. Sometimes we don't hear, and sometimes we don't listen.

11. Running a Spiritual Center

I got a call from the owner of a spiritual center, asking if I wanted to buy the business from him. I agreed and was running it almost immediately. The place was in bad repair and I sank money into renovations. I did the first parts myself but soon decided I needed better skills than mine. I had a new reception area built, rewired the entire place, got new floors throughout, and added a waiting area and a kitchenette.

I ran an open house to re-launch the place and it drew big crowds. True to his word from years before, Paddy McMahon contacted me and offered to give a free talk to help with my launch. That really put the place on the map. The queue for his talk went out the door and down the street. All the therapists, except one, donated time to the open house, and the money paid for their services on the day went towards the cost of the new reception. There was definitely a lot of positive energy flowing that weekend and for some time to come.

I still worked full time as a software engineer and the good pay I received was what financed the renovations. I took out half-page adverts in the phone book in lots of categories and had three phone lines installed. Six months later the new phone book hit the streets and our phones started hopping. I expected a return on my investment would follow but it didn't. I was still hugely out of pocket at the end of each month.

The new booking system I installed allowed me to track everything. The center was busiest in the evenings. Most rooms remained empty during the day. The person with the most clients was Sharon [name changed], the one who did not donate time during the re-launch. Indeed, on the open days she refused to relinquish the room she normally booked, and I had to work around that. Still her room rentals were the main income in the center so I bit my tongue.

For two years the center continued to make a whopping loss. The therapists made better money than before but most were barely keeping their heads above water. Advertising was my biggest expense, and I was caught in a contract with the phone company until the new books came out. I tried increasing the number of therapists but it didn't help. New therapists complained that they weren't making enough money and that I needed to advertise more!

There was a lot of bickering between therapists and a clique formed. Sharon controlled the clique and the receptionist was her sister. They threatened to move to another center unless I got rid of a spiritual healer and reader they didn't like. They also prevented me from letting Dympna, who I adored, work from my center. All these years later I still feel terrible for asking the spiritual healer to leave. She didn't have a bad bone in her body and definitely had both the center's and my best interests at heart.

Lesson learned: Having a skill in the spiritual field is just like being able to ride a bike. It does not mean the person with the skill is not selfish or would not push others out for personal gain.

The Center Becomes Profitable

I finally decided enough was enough. I needed to stop the hemorrhage. Sharon, just one therapist, was making over £90,000 a year. Before I took over she was making around £35,000. My advertising and management style was funneling money into other people's pockets and out of mine! I let my advertising contracts with radio stations and the phone book expire and announced a scaling down. The receptionist was now my biggest expense and I told her I had to let her go and would be installing an automated phone system. She offered to work for free managing the phones while her sister was working. I knew I needed to fully control the center or I would never turn it around. I refused. The shit hit the fan!

Her sister Sharon, the one with the most clients and therefore generating the most income for the center, said she would leave if I followed through. I had no choice but to follow through. I was losing over £20,000 per year, and with the hours I put in at the center, I was effectively working two full-time jobs.

With the new automated system, I didn't need to be there. Therapists were all given keys to let themselves in and were now responsible for managing their own clients. When clients phoned, a voice system guided them to leave a message for a particular therapist. The system then immediately phoned that therapist and played the message to them. The therapist handled the booking from that point. It worked!

The results were astonishing. With Sharon gone I expected to lose even more money. There were now only five therapists left in the center, but all their bookings jumped. Marnie also got a lot more clients and that made the biggest difference. Instead of merely making room rental fees, with Marnie we made direct client fees – five times the amount. The therapists still using the center were now able to make a living from their client bookings. Lest you think we were getting Sharon's clients, that wasn't the case. The automated system didn't take bookings for her but did alert callers that Sharon had moved to another center and provided her new number.

With far fewer therapists, room rentals now paid all the center's bills! Cleaning costs, kitchen supplies, bathroom supplies, and wear and tear costs lowered significantly. I prioritized the course room to suit my bookings so I could run courses whenever I wanted. Finally, the center was supporting me rather than the other way around.

Lesson learned: Keep sight of why you take something on. I focused on making others successful rather than myself. Don't dim your light so others appear to shine brighter.

12. House Problems

Clearing Spirits From My House

My sister, Sally, had appeared on TV3 several times doing ghost busting. Each week the show featured a haunted house, a historian familiar with the locality, Sally the ghost buster, and a psychic. It was very well produced. Sally would be brought to the location and tune in to see what ghosts she could pick up. She would then detail for the viewer what she had seen, what time period the ghost came from, and anything the ghost might have said to her. That was then cross-referenced on the show with what the owners experienced. The historian would delve into what had happened in the house and the locality. Fascinating stuff. Sally always moved them to the light as part of the show. She actually didn't need to be in the physical location to tune in to the ghosts, but it made for good TV.

I lived in Cork for a few years and while there I rented out my Dublin home. I had just recently returned to it. I phoned Sally and asked her to clear the house – just in case. She called me back a few minutes later to say that when she tuned in, she could see my house from the street, but as soon as she turned into my driveway she got lost in a white mist and couldn't find the doorway. The door was only thirty feet from the street so that was surprising. She said she had tried it several times and figured I had a protection around the house.

I was fascinated. With the help of my guides I had indeed put a shield around my house. That was many years earlier. This was proof that it worked. I simply asked my guides to allow Sally through the shield. From that point on she had no problem and sure enough had to move some spirits on.

Lesson learned: Protections work. However, if you give permission for someone to use your premises, they can invite spirits into that space, regardless of the protection you have in place.

Spirits Return When Called Back

After her TV3 exposure, Sally offered ghost busting as a professional service, but more often than not didn't charge money for it. She learned over time that a person who has a problem with spirits is often a wannabe psychic who has done something to attract the negative spirits. They also often have a negative attitude to life, which makes them more likely to attract negative spirits when doing anything psychic.

On a few occasions Sally was called to clear a house again because the spirits had returned. Each time this happened it was because the client had tuned in to the spirits to see if they were indeed gone. That tuning in was their invitation to return.

Lesson learned: If you get someone to clear spirits from your personal space DO NOT tune into it or them to check if they are gone. Trust that they are gone, and as hard as it is, just leave it at that.

Some Predicaments Are Needed

My friend Rachel wanted to move to Cork with her family. She owned her home in Dublin but it had a high mortgage. By selling and moving to Cork she could afford a bigger house with no mortgage. I was saddened to hear she wanted to move. We visited each other often and her sons were my sons' best friends. They would miss each other a lot. I could see the logic in the move and it helped that her husband was from the area they were moving to, but something bothered me about it so I checked with my guides.

I visited her and told her she was not meant to move to Cork. Once I started talking it was like someone got inside my body and completed my sentences. I told her that it took her guides a long time to get her into the financial stress she was in. She needed to be at that stress point because it evoked a feeling in her that was required for her to achieve her life purpose. If she moved, it would take time, but her guides would drip away all the money from the sale until she had the same financial burden. It was part of their promise to her before she incarnated. Their advice was that she enjoyed Dublin more so she may as well be broke there.

As I passed on my message I saw Rachel sitting at her kitchen table in Cork with rolls and rolls of fat on her. I shared that with her too. We both half laughed at that because Rachel was a black belt karate instructor and thin as a rake! She'd never been overweight in her life.

Rachel reasoned she would clear so much money by selling her house in Dublin that she would have money left over after buying a house in Cork. I couldn't argue with that point. Then with her husband's army pension they would always have enough money to sustain themselves, even if he didn't get a job.

She moved a few months later.

A few years after that, I sat in Rachel's kitchen in Cork and with sadness we reviewed how things had turned out. She was wearing the rolls of fat her guides had predicted. Her house had sold well in Dublin and she paid starting money to get a house built in Cork. Then things started to go wrong. Planning permission was denied and they couldn't get their considerable starting money back. They had further problems and lost more money on a second site. Then a third! This happened over a few years and they rented the whole time. Their money was dwindling. By the time they got a house built they had to get a mortgage to complete it. Financially she was no better off.

I can say all this now because Rachel has turned it around. She is slim again and is now following her path and writing.

Lessons learned: Sometimes the predicament we rail against is necessary in our lives. Also, I can channel. Trust it!

13. I Write My First Book

Paddy McMahon organized a reading for me with Maura Lundburg. I had only met her by reputation but was thrilled. Maura explained that she reads auras and would have to close her eyes to see mine. She took a while to begin talking and started with, "I wondered where you got your dream interpretation ability from." I didn't know where, other than from George, so it was interesting to hear. She explained that I was part of a group looking for the Fountain of Youth in a former life. The lifetime was over 300,000 years ago when hominoids had both sex organs and chose the gender they wanted to identify as. I didn't know those hominoids ever existed but listened on. I was in close contact with others in the group now and that was important, as it was to allow me to clear karma with them.

The Fountain of Youth was knowledge, and we took it in turns to go to the spirit world to bring back knowledge. On the fateful occasion it was my turn. I left my body for the spirit world, and my partner, who was having an affair with another member of the group, put metal rods into my body to trap me there. The rods prevented me from returning to my body.

Apparently being trapped on the astral plane for years taught me to interpret dreams. Eventually someone felt remorse and removed the rods. I returned to my body but got septicemia and died quickly. Maura identified three people in the group, including the main culprits. Interestingly each of these people shared a common dislike of, if not hatred, for me. That had never made sense because I'd never done anything to any of them (in this lifetime) and I don't normally get that reaction from anyone.

Leaving the First One

One of them was my boss at the time. I was ten years with Bank of Ireland and a new person had recently replaced the boss in our group. We clashed but now I knew why. I was at work about five weeks after the reading when Marnie phoned with a channeled message. She told me I needed to quit work in order to break free of the past-life connection with my boss. The thought of quitting work scared me, but it had been on my mind since the reading with Maura and I had already had an interview so knew there were other jobs out there. I resigned there and then. In two weeks I was free. It was December 2006.

Several things helped me act on Maura's reading. She had Paddy McMahon's endorsement. That would have been enough for me but her reading also managed to connect the dots between what appeared to be vastly divergent happenings in my life. I also got the buzzing in my crown chakra that told me she was channeling during the reading. Another large influencer was that two weeks after the reading I saw a program on BBC TV about the early hominoids she talked about, so they were indeed real. Lastly, it wasn't going to hurt me to distance myself from people who made it their mission to be jerks in my life!

I'm Nudged to Write

I planned on using my software engineering skills to develop something on my own, but just six days after I resigned I was approached by Skyhorse Publishing in New York and asked to write a book about dream interpretation. The coincidence was amazing. For the first time in twenty years I was free from the pressures of work and had the time to undertake such a project. I was asked to submit a chapter for review. I figured a publisher's main interest would be in a symbol dictionary but I never liked them. I set about fixing that by writing a dictionary that was based on actual dreams I'd analyzed. I picked a letter at random and wrote entries beginning with 'B'. I also wrote an educational chapter about the heart. Six weeks after I was contacted, I sent my sample to the publisher. I knew it was good.

I didn't hear back for a couple of days so I phoned and was informed that they had already agreed to a contract with another writer. I was gutted and the bad feeling easily lasted two weeks. I knew from my own work that this is often how guides put you on your path. The publisher contacting me at precisely the right time merely gave me the nudge I needed. I was still happy with what I had written so decided to finish the book.

I had been writing an educational newsletter as part of my website for a few years. I had all my newsletters and the dreams I'd analyzed in them to draw from. I was free to write a book exactly how I wanted, unencumbered by a publisher's requirements. With so much material I was sure it would only take me about three months. I was wrong – it took nine!

Writing a book was far more difficult than writing a newsletter. I had to dig far deeper into each topic than I had previously done. I also had to check and recheck the dreams I used for illustration in the book. At times the writing was very slow indeed. There were days when I just pushed the cursor around the screen. I'd want to write about one topic but only got thoughts on another. One time, the inspiration on a different topic was so strong I decided to jot down the thoughts in my head for later. Instead of writing notes, I watched the beginnings of a fully formed chapter flow onto the page. It was the most valuable lesson I learned in writing. I needed to get out of my own way and write what was coming to me rather than what I had previously planned.

Using that method, the book flowed and I knew I was in harmony with what I was meant to be doing. I began to meditate prior to writing and could feel my guides comment as I wrote. If I got something wrong I knew it, and could check with them until I fixed the error. By the time I completed the book my channeling had improved enormously. By the time it was published, I had added fuel to my passion for dream analysis.

I finished my first book, *How To Interpret Your Dreams And Discover Your Life Purpose,* in September 2007. I decided to self-publish. I bought the book's ISBN from Neilson and spent €12,000 on two thousand lithographic color copies. This was before the days of Kindle. I was thrilled with both the quality and the content of the book. Today, it is still something I am proud to have done.

Lesson learned: Always write what is flowing. Don't compromise on quality. Spend money on what you believe in.

Marketing My Book

I sold the book through my newsletter and my website. I couldn't find an interested distributor in Ireland so I personally visited bookstores and asked them to order copies. Most did, but there were many awkward and some costly experiences. It was a slog. Some bookstores never paid me for what they had sold. Others would only order from a distributor. Some of the rejections were for surprising reasons. One owner refused because the book had the 'C' word. She couldn't even say the word cancer! Hodges Figgis on Dawson Street gave the most ludicrous reason for refusal. In a bookstore with seven floors and tens of thousands of books, the manager asked me what my qualifications for writing the book were. I wondered if she asked that of every author on her shelves, or indeed any other author. This route was not going to work. As ironic as it sounds, I began to feel that bookstores in Ireland didn't like authors.

I considered ordering the book in Hodges Figgis. Censorship is illegal, so they would have to order a copy from me, but that wouldn't guarantee they would order extra copies to hold on their shelves.

One of the easiest experiences I had in Ireland was with Waterstones, an English-owned bookstore chain. The manager in the first Waterstones I approached simply looked at the quality of the book and said, "Yes." He wished me well with the book and told me where their other outlets were, and said they would take some too. Indeed, they did. Based on that, I decided to fly to London and try bookstores there. I figured it couldn't be worse than Ireland.

I spent three days walking to bookstores around London. I had ten targets before travelling and eight of them took copies. So did other bookstores I encountered, but London did not have as many small bookstores as Ireland. Each store that took it was like the Waterstones in Ireland. Their main criteria for carrying it were quality, subject and terms. I had faith again that bookstores do like authors – just not in Ireland.

Since Ireland was my main market and most of the big bookstores would only deal with a distributor, I needed to find one. I researched but could not find anything appropriate in Ireland. They all expected the publisher (in my case, me) to carry the full risk for bad debts and damaged returns. Since I had already experienced several bookstores that had sold my books but subsequently refused to pay invoices, I couldn't agree to that. I did strike a deal with Gardners in England. They distributed worldwide but not in my market (Ireland)!

Selling through my website was still my best option. I lowered my list price to offset the cost of shipping so that buying from my website would match bookstore prices. My aim was to help sales but it didn't. Instead it annoyed some of the bookstores I was already dealing with.

A year later my brother Joe came to my rescue. He put me in touch with

Columba Mercier Distribution, a distributor that handled everything for 17% of the cover price. They took the risk for non-payment and returns too. The agent assigned to me explained that they controlled so many titles that bookstores eventually paid their invoices or got struck off. I signed contracts and delivered half my books to their warehouse. It was still up to me to promote my book to create orders, and to pay for it to be listed on the POS system used by bookstores. But at least now I could simply tell my website readers to order my book in any bookstore!

This arrangement worked until a few years later when the distributor merged with another and costs jumped.

Although there was a lot of heartache involved in trying to get my book into bookstores it was not all bad. Certain bookstores were extremely accommodating and I kept a personal relationship with them even after I had a distributor. These stores continuously sold lots of copies.

Along Comes Kindle

When Kindle hit Ireland, I bought one with the intention of formatting my book for it. I spent a few weeks using the software tools in their publishing suite, testing what worked and what didn't work on their various readers. I needed the dictionary to be searchable. Pretty soon my book was available on Amazon, albeit only in digital format.

In my view, the closed cartel of publishers, distributors and large bookstores, along with their high margins, paved the way for Kindle to take off. Ignoring costs during writing, self-publishing is still very costly. A book that sells for $10 only makes a few cents profit for the author when printing, distribution and bookstore costs are paid. The same book selling for $3 on Kindle yields a profit of up to $2 for the author. The reader and the author are both better off!

Kindle opened the book market to authors, the content creators behind all books.

Lesson learned: Do what your heart says. Don't focus too much on revenue. Avenues for selling my book exist now that didn't exist when I wrote it.

14. Slieve na Calliagh

My energy was in a slump that I couldn't seem to shift. My friend, Seán, offered to bring me to Slieve na Calliagh, a Stone Age site, to fix me. He had been there recently and it had totally recharged him. I'd nothing to lose, especially given my interest in Stone Age sites! Plus, I'd never been there before.

Slieve na Calliagh is a 6,000-year-old site in County Meath, and fairly remote. You have to leave the road and walk two kilometers to get to it. It's more like a hike as you climb five hundred feet in elevation on that walk. Once you get there it is immediately impressive. The huge cairn is aligned to the sunrise on the equinox but there are dozens of different stations (monuments) scattered around it.

Seán used his pendulum to determine which stations I required, and the precise order in which to visit them. I stood at the first one and felt energy being pulled from me. I hadn't expected that. This place was still active! My energy was being drained but very precisely, so I stayed there and let it happen.

When instructed by the pendulum, we moved to the next one. Here I felt energy moving through me but particularly at one chakra. I tuned in to my guides and was told the place was like a spiritual hospital. Each station did something different with your energy. Some cleared chakras to remove blockages, some balanced energy once blockages were cleared, and others charged you by injecting energy.

We visited nine of the stations and I was feeling great at the end of it. I could feel each one working on me. When we were done, the pendulum directed us to face the large cairn to give thanks. I could see three spirits looking at us. This was amazing. These spirits were here working the structure for our benefit! We thanked them and walked back to the car.

I was rejuvenated and stayed that way. However, when I talked to Seán a few days later, he said he had gone back to Slieve na Calliagh. He was feeling terrible since our visit and when he channeled on it, was told that he should not have stood with me at each station. The path he had asked for, and the path given, was to heal me. In the process he had exposed himself to energy that had unbalanced him. When he returned he was guided to take the path he required.

Lesson learned: Some Stone Age sites are still active and manned (by spirits). Check with your guides that it is okay to walk around a Stone Age site and only follow the path they approve.

15. Moving to Seattle

In December 2010, my daughter Heidi offered to donate a kidney to her uncle in Alaska. He had been on dialysis for years. Heidi could channel better than me but she asked me to channel on it. I got that she'd be a match. She was very nervous about it and so was I. We talked about it a lot. It would take a year for tests to confirm compatibility and she could withdraw her offer at any time, right up until and including when she was on the operating table.

Heidi had wanted to move to America for some time, I suspect mostly because she was born there. She asked if I would consider the whole family moving. For some reason it just seemed like a good idea to me. I had previously lived in America for five years and really liked it. Marnie had wanted to move back several times but at those times I knew Ireland had more to offer me. When Heidi asked, I knew that Ireland had given me all it could.

Of my four children, three were open to moving. My eldest son, Karl, was in college and in a relationship with the love of his life. I knew he'd want to stay in Ireland. Marnie was living on her own in Cork. She took very little convincing and was soon on board.

Having American citizenship removed all red tape around Heidi's offer to donate her kidney. Dates were set for her to travel to America for further compatibility testing. Meanwhile, I applied for a green card. I had one previously and naïvely thought it would simply be a matter of requesting that back. It wasn't. I had to reapply. I filled out all the paperwork, did all the background checks and mostly just waited. When all hurdles were clear we began selling everything we had, except our two houses.

On July 22, 2011, Heidi and her son Billie, Brian, and Julie boarded a plane to leave Ireland. At just twelve years old, Julie was very brave to do it. She cried going through the departure gate while I pretended to be strong. Once they were out of sight I cried too. They would be in good hands living with their grandmother in Alaska. In early August we were informed that Marnie would not need to attend my interview at the American embassy and she left Ireland to join them.

On September 29, with green card secured, I left Ireland too. Heidi's operation was to be performed in Seattle so I headed straight there. I stayed with my brother-in-law, Art, while I searched for accommodation. Two weeks later Art helped me move to my own place and the rest of my family in America joined me from Alaska. It was a happy reunion. It felt like a year had gone by rather than ten weeks. Julie transferred from middle school in Fairbanks to Seattle. It was her second school move that year and her fourth in ten months! All were due to moving address.

I felt really lucky to find the house I was renting. I had no credit history or credit score and wanted to move in immediately – all the signs that trigger alarm bells! I knew the agent was on board from the beginning though. Within three days I had the keys and Internet hooked up. I was still working for my brother in Ireland. Our client was in America and I needed to dial in to their systems for work so a good Internet connection was essential.

Heidi Goes Under the Knife

In January 2012 Heidi went through with the kidney donation. Six weeks later she was mobile again and in March she left for Alaska. Originally I had expected to only stay in Seattle until after the operation, and then choose where I wanted to live, but I really liked Seattle. I decided to rekindle my dream work here. I looked up a local dream group and signed up. It took two buses each way to get to it but I knew I also needed to get out of the house.

Jaime Dyson led the group on my first night and I immediately warmed to her. Her energy was very honest. I struck up a conversation with the intention of asking if she thought her group would be interested in doing my six-week class but she informed me she was not the group leader so I didn't ask. The following week I met Susan Pullen. Her energy was harder to read than Jaime's and I didn't know how my offer would be received, so I held back yet again. I wanted to test run my course in Seattle. If it was received well by a group of dream experts in America, then it would be received well in general. With them, I would quickly discover any hardline attitudes I might encounter. I resolved to ask at the next session.

My First Class in Seattle

The following week it was Jaime leading again. I gave her a copy of my book and asked if she would discuss with Susan the idea of me doing the six-week class. The offer was received favorably, and Susan, Jaime and several from their group did my course. Susan and Jaime gave me great feedback at the end of the six weeks and with a little tinkering around the edges I was confident my course was America-ready.

I continued to attend their weekly dream group. Early on, a core participant who hadn't done my class took a dislike to me. She could hardly hide her venom and even walked out one week. Due to her hostility I remained silent most of the time, just interpreting dreams to myself. I made an exception if the dream belonged to Susan or Jaime or if it gave a health warning.

I enjoyed attending the group and stayed in it for over three years. Some of the analyses offered were very insightful, especially by a spritely woman by the name of Colleen.

Seattle Channeling Group

Jaime started a splinter group with a focus on lucid dreams, meeting on Tuesdays in south Seattle. Lucid dreams were not my forte but I offered my support and attended each session. Frequently, it was just me, Jaime and Katherine, and the discussion would drift to talking about guides rather than dreams. Jaime pestered me to teach them how to channel. I truthfully told them I couldn't but I could show them the techniques we used in Ireland.

We met the following Wednesday. I had only intended showing the techniques on that one night, but I so thoroughly enjoyed the experience and working with energies again that I agreed to meet regularly. It helped that my guides pushed me to keep it up too. After meeting a few times, Susan joined our group.

We followed the same strategy as in my first channeling group, to create a protected space around the channel. Whoever wasn't channeling sent energy from their heart chakra to the crown chakra of the channel. Sending energy is done by imagining a beam of love going to the target. It sounds easy to do, but more often than not it gets sent from the wrong chakra, or is very weak. I enjoyed looking at the beam and directing the sender to open up more or move it to the correct chakra. It had been some time since I got to play with that.

Within a few months everyone in the group was channeling. We didn't get any earth-bound souls this time. On one occasion it was Katherine's turn. When I tried sending energy to her it was not accepted. I looked at her aura and she had a huge shell around herself. It came from within, swelled up and out from her crown chakra and then down around her whole body. I could see there was no block on the center of her crown chakra and was able to send my beam there to establish the connection. When quizzed about it, she said she had been channeling on her own during the week and had a very unpleasant experience. She didn't like the answer she was given to a question and in a panic she put up a force field to protect herself. It was interesting to see that force field became real and to see its effectiveness against me making a connection. I told her she had left an opening though. The next time we met, Katherine's protective shield was gone. I never asked if she removed it or if it just diminished on its own.

In the early days of our group, I offered to interpret a dozen dreams for each member, one person per session. It went well until it was time to do Katherine's dreams. I established my connection and began interpreting the dreams she had given to me. It was an interactive session and on the first dream Katherine casually mentioned that she didn't believe my method. Normally that would have deflated me and I would have lost my connection, but I determined to persevere. I completed the full set. I was still bewildered at her comment but was thrilled that I kept my connection alive and took that as a turning point for me.

I discussed Katherine's comment with Susan the following day and she clarified that Katherine was referring to something I had said about guides. It wasn't about my dream analysis method! I found that amusing. In either case I had grown as a result of the experience.

Over time, as people became comfortable with their connections, we no longer needed to create the protected space for each other. We also changed the format and started bringing serious questions to the group. Three years later we still meet every two weeks. Jaime moved to Texas so we include her over Skype. It has been a blessing for me by providing a constant positive spiritual development group in addition to the guidance channeled for me by the members of the group.

Lessons learned: With practice, a connection can be maintained even in what you perceive as a hostile environment. Also, get into a spiritual development group and stay in it. Grow with the group and allow it to change.

Guides Are Here on the Planet

The year I came to Seattle I was asked by Miki Strong to be part of a Purpose to Profits weeklong suite of presentations. As part of it I offered to analyze dreams from participants. One stood out. The dream came from Denise in Australia, and the analysis was amazing. Part of my analysis is given here:

> *You are a spiritual being, here to lead and heal. You are here to oversee the tearing down of the dominant male energy in society and the transition of society into unconditional love, open minds and enlightened thinking. Your transition onto this path will be sudden and assured. You will know how to help others because you forced yourself to live their path so that you could relate. You will do this on an international scale. Your healing is not aimed at one-to-one. It is healing on a global scale.*

I had encountered guides through dreams before, but it seemed like I had met the queen bee. Denise's response was that the global nature made sense. I then thought about other guides for whom I had analyzed dreams, looking for similar global messages. Two stood out. In both cases their dreams included symbols of the earth 'wobbling'. At that point the guide would focus on bringing a new spiritual power onto the earth plane. Two people had the same dreams with the same meaning, years apart and in different locations. It reminded me of my encounter with Pearson Walker Beavis all those years ago.

Lesson learned: There is a consistency of purpose among guides who are here on the planet.

16. The Whidbey Island Succubus

I stayed in a friend's house on Whidbey Island. Our introduction was by the clairvoyant I had my very first reading with, Brendan O'Callaghan. He had recently started an online Facebook group and when he learned I moved to Seattle, he connected me with two of his members, Joanna and Dan. I had been to their house a few months earlier with Brian and Julie, and they had invited me back to spend the night. I took them up on their offer.

Their rented house was what Americans call a rambler – all on one level. Joanna had a glass workshop on the property but due to ill health had not worked in it for some years. On my last visit she showed her workshop to Brian and Julie. They were very impressed and Joanna sent them home with a book of high-resolution pictures of glass art work. The intention was that they each pick a piece from the book, and she'd help them make it in her workshop on a subsequent visit. Although glass art is not my thing, the pieces in her house and in her book were stunning. I think it is the inner child in us drawn to objects that sparkle. Look! A squirrel!

Like the last time, I rented a car for the trip as there is no other way to get there. It involves a one-hour drive from north Seattle, taking the Whidbey ferry, and a further thirty-five-minute drive on Whidbey Island. I enjoyed the drive for many reasons. It was my first time away overnight since moving to Seattle. Then there was the sense of achievement of being on the other side of the world and navigating my way to a destination that was definitely tricky to get to.

The evening with Joanna and Dan was lovely, with the exception of being introduced to their dogs. They each had one. Dog lovers have no concept of what it is like for a non-dog-lover to have them included at the table. Dogs sense that I don't like them and every once in a while one will try to win me over by licking my hand or nudging me. I don't like either action. To me it is the same as a stranger licking my hand – weird and uncalled for. The fact that it is another species adds to the insult, but it is the teeth designed to rip my flesh apart that really make me feel uncomfortable. That's the part that amuses a dog lover. For them there is never any need to be uncomfortable around a dog, but I know a dog can sense my fear and that makes the dog uncomfortable and on guard around me. I know it is my input into the mix of feelings that sours the situation, but I have not found the off switch for it yet, and at this point in my life I have to assume I was born without one. I also am not calmed by the rhetorical reassurance from a dog's owner. They think I am calm but the fear is just pushed below my pores and the dog can smell it.

There are two occasions when I was reassured by an owner that their dog wouldn't bite me but their dog failed to listen. I got three things from each time it happened – conviction that I'm right not to trust dogs, or the owner's word that their dog doesn't bite, and a tetanus shot.

When we retired for the evening I was interested to see what I would sense in the way of spirits or energy. Joanna had told me that there was negative energy in the house, and that her uncle, a Native American spiritual leader, had performed ceremonies to try dislodging it but it remained. This was the reason I went there without my daughter. I didn't want her to have a bad experience. My son at this point was already well versed in spirits and energy and would have welcomed any experience. However, he couldn't come without my daughter coming, and I wasn't going to have her spend a night in the house. Before falling asleep I tuned in to the energy in the room. I thought I detected her uncle's charm running through a beam below the roof and that felt good. It was more like a flow of red energy than a pin-point location but I knew it was intended to help. I bravely turned off the lights and fell asleep.

Hours later I awoke to a grunting sound like a pig makes when eating. I was lying on my stomach. At the same time, I also felt something nuzzling into the back of my neck on my left side. The physical sensation was quite strong but not unpleasant. I realized the something was not physical and for a while I wondered whether I should ignore it. When I realized it was not going away I lifted the upper half of my body off the bed and pushed at the something to move it away. It moved to the top of the nightstand beside my bed. It looked like Joanna's small dog but hadn't quite got the copying correct. Its features were rubbery and its neck was like a vacuum cleaner hose but wider. I could tell the neck stretched and indeed the entity was having trouble maintaining its shape especially around the neck. After my initial shock and questioning out loud, "What the heck are you?" I was pleased to notice that my fear did not build and instead I was amused at this new spirit. I had never seen one of these before. It sat on the night stand trying its best to remain still and look like Joanna's dog. It failed at both. My amusement was because in its ignorance it had assumed the form of Joanna's dog in order to get close to me without raising my alarm! Clearly it had not tuned in to me at the table earlier in the night. I knew where it stood on the intelligence scale.

I watched it for a few minutes. I turned on the light to bring myself out of the state where I could see it and a short while later turned it off again to go back to sleep. It came back to the same spot in my neck. I say in my neck because it was deep below the skin. Its connection was not as strong this time and I asked my guides to make sure I was as protected as I needed to be. I slept through the rest of the night without any event that I was aware of.

I never mentioned my experience to Joanna. I didn't see the point. She already knew there was bad energy there. I was glad I didn't bring my daughter though, and I wondered if Joanna's illness was related to the entity. I'm sure it was trying to suck energy from me. I think it was initially getting some and that is what woke me up. It felt like a tickle in my neck – on the inside, about an inch and a half below my skin. Almost a pleasant feeling!

Lesson learned: The succubus is real! Some spirits do attack you in the night. However, you have to be open (a channel) for this to happen. If you're a channel, it is part of your contract to learn how to protect your energy. If you don't develop your channeling ability – these negative entities still see you.

After breakfast, Joanna and Dan drove me around Whidbey looking for places I could rent to do workshops, and for bookshops to take my book. If I got my book into a bookshop, then people would look for courses from me. Right? In some parallel universe, where everything goes to plan, my other self is sipping piña coladas between sold out courses! I enjoyed a very pleasant morning and afternoon going to three bookshops and two possible event venues. In one, the bookshop clerk wanted me to come back because the owner was not there. Another was the wrong type of bookshop, but the third was perfect. The owner, however, was clearly unwell. When Joanna introduced me to her, I immediately felt her connect with her guides through her brow chakra – a fantastic sign to me that she is the real deal. I jokingly told her I caught her checking on me but before I finished my sentence she had to rush to the restroom to vomit! When she came back you could tell she was just barely keeping it together to not vomit on customers. She asked me to come back when she was over her illness! We did look at two very nice places to run workshops though and I liked the draw of a retreat on the island.

My time was up and I had to return to the mainland. I hugged Joanna and Dan and drove back to the ferry.

Lesson learned: I wasn't pushing against closed doors! It's okay when things don't work out the way you want.

17. Meeting Sandy

I bought a ticket to a dream interpretation event in Kirkland. Some months before, I had discovered a lady based in Seattle who promoted herself as The Dream Detective. I wrote to her but never got a reply. Two months later, I discovered she was booked to talk at a singles event where she claimed she could help people find their ideal partner from analyzing their dreams. This interested me because from my experience, while it is common for dreams to comment on relationships, they only tell you why you keep picking 'that' type of person and how to stop that. They don't help you with who you should pick. It was entirely possible I was going to learn something new.

I printed out directions from Google Maps to and from the event location. As is common, I found the vicinity of the event easily enough and then spiraled in on the exact location. By that I mean I slowly passed it going in opposite directions each time by less and less until I figured out where it had to be. I pulled in to the car park and stood by the trunk of my car. People had started arriving and were forming small groups while waiting for the doors to open. I began to get alarmed when I saw how well everyone was dressed. It was hitting me that this was a singles event after all, and while I was only interested in the dream segment I wondered if I'd find myself thrown in at the deep end and have to introduce myself to seasoned singles event goers. I'm sure there is a technical term for those people but not knowing it just shows how out of my league I was feeling.

The event organizer arrived and discovered the doors were locked and no key was available. Renessa is an amazing person. If you ever plan on getting stranded on a remote island, make sure Renessa is with you. She won't settle for being stuck, so she'll either get you all off the island in double quick time, or turn things around so that the rest of the planet will pay top dollar to come visit your exotic location. While keeping everyone informed, Renessa quickly ran through all the options for gaining access or using another local venue. Nothing worked so she booked a room in a luxury restaurant in Bellevue, some seven miles away. Just after she booked another car pulled in to the lot. It was driven by a person who immediately reminded me of the character played by Whoopi Goldberg in "Sister Act" – a conspicuous person designed to stick out! Sandy had just entered stage left.

It was clear Renessa knew her and she asked her to drive ahead of everyone to show us the way to the new venue in Bellevue. Sandy obliged but hopped into her car and sped off so quickly that only three cars got to follow her. I was one of them. However, being new to driving in Seattle, I stuck to the speed limit and soon was lost behind them. I was coming to a major intersection and trying to guess which way they may have gone when I was beckoned by another car that had also been lost by Sandy but knew the way. Course corrected, I followed them to the venue. It occurred to me on the way that I had little chance of finding my way home with my map from Kirkland. I hoped this was going to be worth it.

My new trailblazer also knew the restaurant so I followed her into a car park and in we went. We were led to a large room that was hastily being set up with tables organized in a large U-shape. I sat beside the trailblazer and enjoyed conversation while we waited for everyone else. Renessa, who had stayed in Kirkland to inform the last stragglers of the changed location, was last to arrive. She immediately asked that the U-formation be turned to face the other way. In the scuffle I lost my new companion and ended up sitting between Sandy and a lady named Linda. The event formally began.

Renessa talked about the law of attraction and how mindset, and focus on what can go wrong, is often the cause of a single person's strike-out at singles events and events in general. She was such a good speaker I took notes. I didn't have to write down everything she said because, as it turned out, she was describing my mindset and luck with women. I had the advantage of experience while others had to take copious notes. I wasn't looking for a relationship. I was eleven years separated, despite many pushes from friends. Still, Renessa was filled with wisdom and willing to share. It just makes sense to sit up and pay attention when a seriously good-looking woman is telling you how to attract a woman like her! That's not how she was putting it of course but I was reading between the lines.

The Dream Detective was invited to talk and I agreed in general with everything she said. However, she never said how dreams help you find a partner. That was the piece I wanted to hear and my whole reason for being there. When the dream segment ended, Renessa took over and had us do the very thing I didn't want to happen. We were instructed to turn to the person on our left and cringe, cringe, cringe. Okay, it was more like tell them five things about yourself, but I was still reading between the lines. So I had fifteen minutes of cringing with Linda and then we wrapped up. I didn't score but like I said, I didn't even know there was a target. At least I was still alive and the dying only happened to a part of me on the inside.

As I was collecting my things Sandy introduced herself. She was sitting to my right the whole time but we didn't even get to acknowledge each other. She asked me what I thought of the event. To fend off another dismal performance on my part, I told her I had only come for the segment on dreams, but that overall I was surprised at how much I got out of it. I then asked her if she was a rally driver as I was in a sports car but she still lost me on the way to the event. We had a laugh about that and some other things but the point is the event was over. We were no longer in pick-up mode so I was safe – or so I thought. Cue the music for "Jaws" in the background!

Sandy was very easy to talk to. I learned later that this is because she loves to talk. Getting her to be quiet is the trick but how was I to know that? So there were no pregnant pauses in our conversation. To this day she still doesn't know that pregnant pauses exist, but at the time it meant that, so very easily, we were engrossed in conversation. I told her I was new to Seattle. She suggested I go see the King Tut exhibition at the Space Needle. We talked some more. She said she'd be interested in going to see the King Tut exhibition. We talked some more. Staff started clearing us out and then, although I still don't know how it works, Renessa's lessons formed a fist and punched me in the brain. "Would you like to go see the King Tut exhibition with me?" I had just asked Sandy on a date! Yes, the astute reader will notice that she asked me twice, and first, but let's not be petty.

We exchanged numbers and as we were heading back to the cars I explained my dilemma of not knowing where I was or how to get home. She generously offered to drive in my direction until I got to my exit off the interstate. With enough pleading from me, she was careful not to lose me and pretty soon I began recognizing where I was. After waving and pulling off towards my house I smiled at the thought that the first time I ever went to a singles event a beautiful woman brought me home!

We Start Dating

Sandy and I went on our date. The exhibit was amazing, but we quickly realized we hadn't the slightest interest in, or knowledge of, King Tut. Rather than feign interest, we were honest with each other and moved to a café beside the exhibit. Conversation was still effortless between us. We were only there for fifteen minutes but that was enough time for Sandy to show her trademark calling card – she knocked her iced tea over! Two weeks later I'd be getting a borrowed car detailed to remove evidence of the same thing. It's not that she drops every iced tea. She just drinks so many of them that statistically she's bound to drop one on you soon after you meet! We ended our first date at a wonderful butterfly exhibit.

Our second date was better planned. We went to a restaurant. We ate and talked. It was great. We shared the same taste in food. My tastes are plain, so that was a joy to discover. I once had to choke down a dish during an interview and pretend it was delicious. I wouldn't ever have to do that with Sandy! We shared the same tastes in music. Excellent! My only fear was that Sandy might be ten years younger than me and I was so relieved to discover we were close in age.

A surprise to both of us was our mutual interest in the spiritual field. Sandy shared her passion for Abraham Hicks and *The Law of Attraction*. I had never heard of it before the singles event so it was very interesting to hear that perspective. Nothing in it, or in anything she had learned about the spiritual field, conflicted with anything I had learned or experienced. Of course it shouldn't, but it is still nice to see that!

On our third date our relationship became official. A year later we rented a house together. Two years after that, in 2015, we got married. Oh, I forgot to say, "Spoiler Alert!" - I'm jumping ahead.

I Quit Alcohol

Over the course of five months I had three dreams that told me to stop drinking. One said it was blocking my ability to be articulate in writing by limiting the connection with my higher self. (Indeed I was off alcohol for years before I wrote my first book.) Another dream said it would seriously affect my health if I didn't stop.

At that time, I worked from home and Sandy worked for Boeing. Her job required her to be at work for meetings on the east coast, which meant a 6 a.m. start. The consequence was that she went to bed a lot earlier than me. If we were going out for a meal or drinks, we were generally home by 7:30, and then she'd be off to bed. I got into the habit of watching TV and having more drinks until a more reasonable bedtime – not every night, but still too often. The dreams were warranted.

When I was younger I had gone years without drinking alcohol. I knew what that felt like so was determined to get into that space again. I also knew people who hadn't drunk for years, but it was a constant struggle for them. I didn't want that struggle! I looked at the amount of free time I would have if I quit drinking – all the time I had in the evening before I went to bed. What could I do with that? I could write a book. I could push my dream analysis career further, to the point where I made my living through it. I knew a goal was important, as it would support my new aim of not drinking.

I knew the energy I was looking for. I wanted to be able to sit in a restaurant with others who were drinking and not even be thinking about alcohol. It took two attempts to succeed. For me, attempting something at the right time is like riding the crest of a wave. I enjoy the experience of what I'm doing rather than thinking about what I am not doing.

Sandy now enjoys having a designated driver. She just rarely takes me up on it!

Lesson learned: Alcohol limits my abilities. Duh! Goals do the opposite by testing and pushing my abilities. Pursuing goals gives a great sense of achievement and builds a momentum that is not easy to give up.

Shamanic Charms

Sandy and I bought a house in September 2014. One of our fast requirements was that it had to be suitable for running my dream courses. This one was perfect, and we dedicated an entire floor for that purpose. We purchased large conference tables and chairs, installed a wooden floor, new windows, an overhead projector, new toilets and were ready for business.

Susan Pullen, along with our friend and her shamanic mentor, Jacki, performed a shamanic ceremony to bless the new classroom. The ceremony included fixing protective charms to each of the walls.

We started holding our bi-weekly channeling group in the classroom to help the energy. During one of these groups I discovered I couldn't make a connection. This just never happened. In addition to not making a connection, I saw a male spirit moving in my aura. That's so unusual to see. Spirits do not normally make their presence known but this one relished his intrusive nature. I couldn't see what he was doing but I knew he was blocking my connection. Others in the group seemed to have no problem establishing their connections!

The following morning Heidi tuned in to the problem and was told that someone had done an energy clearing on my classroom and also put up a block on anyone making a connection. I knew who it was. I had recently invited an instructor to use my new classroom to hold her Washington course. She was also going to be staying in my house and was due to arrive two days later.

She confirmed she had done the energy clearing. I didn't tell her about the spirit I saw or confront her about clearing my space. The damage was already done. I decided to let her run her class and I would have the problem fixed afterwards. I didn't want her clients to have a bad experience in my classroom. On Sunday, while she was running her class, I had to interpret a client's dream but I couldn't do it without a connection. I sat at my computer one floor above the classroom and tuned in to the energy.

I saw a lattice structure under my house with lots of antennae on it. The antennae were flashing active so I knew something was still good. I could see that the connection with this structure was blocked or more accurately the bottom floor of the house was isolated from it. I had to work so I forged a connection from my computer room down to the lattice structure and then all the way across it. As soon as I did that my connection was back. I did my client's dream and the instructor was none the wiser as far as I know.

She left for the airport two days later and I got Jacki back to fix the energy in the place. From that point on, I would be extremely careful about who I would invite into my classroom space.

Lesson learned: Be careful who you invite into your space. Once invited in, a person can trample on the delicate energy work you've got in place. Interestingly the person does not even need to be physically present!

18. The Inspiration for My Radio Show

I continued to do radio interviews, holding up my end of the bargain to never turn down a show. I had already done a few in 2014 when I was invited onto Highland Radio in Donegal in July. The eight-hour time difference set my interview for just after 2 a.m. I got up, freshened up and waited. At 3:20 a.m. I emailed the producer and was told my slot had been cancelled due to other news items. She rescheduled for the following day. I wanted to cancel but stuck to my promise. Amazingly, the same thing happened the following night. On the third night, I was not so surprised when it happened again. I didn't reschedule.

I had done thousands of radio interviews on many stations and that had never happened before. I decided to make something positive out of it and asked via my website for volunteers who I would interview to create my own podcast. I got a great response and recorded seven interviews in one day and created three podcasts from them. I was really just experimenting and not too sure where I could take it, but it was fun to do. My interviewees got lots of dreams analyzed so it was a win-win but I felt I was missing something and decided not to pursue it further.

In August 2014 I was invited by Trevor, a radio presenter, to be a guest on his show in Seattle on KKNW. This interview was closest to home and scheduled for September. On the morning of the interview, Trevor phoned to say a famous psychic was in town and that he needed to push my interview out two weeks.

Two weeks later, on the morning of my rescheduled interview, I looked up KKNW and found links to Trevor's radio schedule. I wasn't listed, so I phoned him just to check in. This time, he had forgotten about our interview. I knew my guides were trying to tell me something, but I wasn't getting it! Trevor asked to meet on the weekend to discuss the interview in advance. He chose a bookstore close to where I lived. I arrived early and when Trevor was fifteen minutes late I phoned him. He said he was in his car only three miles away. I waited another forty-five minutes and left. He was a no-show.

I went home and checked out KKNW's website again, mainly to look for comments about Trevor. Instead I discovered that they were looking for presenters. The wheels started to turn in my head. Meanwhile, Trevor phoned and scheduled our interview for that Friday. For the next two days I weighed up the pros and cons of doing my own radio show. On Monday I phoned KKNW and set up a meeting to discuss doing a show on dreams.

When I was finally interviewed by Trevor, my own show was already scheduled to start on November 18, in just a few weeks. It was a half hour per week, airing live. I planned on doing callers' dreams, educational segments and dreams that listeners emailed. My short-term goal was to become experienced at presenting and interviewing others. My long-term goal was to get a syndicated TV show.

I titled my show "So, You Think You're Awake?" because our dreams attempt to awaken us to our life purpose. It is ironic that we are rarely closer to discovering the purpose of our life than while we sleep and dream.

My Radio Show Begins

On the morning of my first show I had major jitters. If anyone had witnessed me prepare, they would have thought I was testing a new laxative. I am always nervous before a show but being the presenter brought me to a new level of panic. I would be fully responsible for the success or failure of the show, including any dead air time.

It took three shows before I started to relax. I also had to concentrate on talking more slowly. My regular Irish speed was too brisk. My friend used to joke that if I talked any faster my lips would fly off. Within a few months I had my talking speed under control too.

Twenty weeks in, I scheduled my first interview with Jacki Campbell, the healer and medium who performed the blessing in my classroom. A lot of listeners' dreams referenced channeling so the topic was on point. I could have scheduled my daughter Heidi, since she is an excellent medium, but I thought it more professional to interview outside of my own family. The night before Jacki's scheduled appearance, she cancelled due to bronchitis and Heidi casually offered to stand in for her.

Heidi was a natural at the microphone and the show was a huge success. Listeners even wrote with the opinion that Heidi was meant to be on the show. Eleven weeks later, when my show was increased to one hour, she joined me as a permanent co-host. So too did Susan Pullen. Susan and Heidi brought a new balance to the show. Their presence also allowed for good-natured banter which I'm sure continues to amuse our listeners.

Lessons learned: If something that has always gone smoothly (over twenty years) inexplicably becomes a frustrating issue, it might be an indication that it is time for you to move to the next level. My frustration with being a radio show guest opened the door to me becoming a radio show host.

19. Full Immersion Into Spirit

Elizabeth Rose, or Liz, sent me a dream to analyze in 2007. I receive many dream requests and normally record or type the analysis but for some reason I wrote to Liz and asked her if I could call her and analyze it over the phone. We did. That was a first for me but I knew it was the way to do it.

We exchanged emails from time to time after that and Liz became a hypnotist, partly as a result of my analysis. During her course she became fascinated with regressions as a way of healing traumas. That made sense, as her dreams told her she needed to heal a trauma from which she had no conscious memory and hypnosis had enabled her to do it.

In 2013 she visited me in Seattle and we swapped sessions. She regressed me and I analyzed her dreams. It was fun catching up but I knew she was after something with the regressions. She was just too keen to regress me and then she'd want to do it again immediately. Shortly after she returned home to Canada she became able to trance channel. She was very excited about it and so was I.

In 2015 she reached a new level with regressions and informed me that my guides wanted me to come to Canada for three days so she could work on me. I checked with my guides and they confirmed it. That was a surprise. We set a date but I didn't buy any tickets. I was due to get married and thought I'd put the trip to Canada off until the next year. As the time grew closer my guides got louder and louder about how important the experience was for me. With less than a week to go, I relented and purchased my flights at a now very inflated price.

Liz aptly titled her new course, "Full Immersion Into Spirit." I had high hopes for the trip based on how much my guides endorsed it, but what I got was stunning. Liz wanted to fix me on a few fronts. A few months prior to travelling, she got me to drop meat and sugar from my diet. She said it would help me reach a deeper level during the regressions.

We started each morning with vegetarian food. Yum! Makes you want to jump out of bed. That was followed by an hour of yoga. Liz would go into trance and allow her guides to direct the postures. I was carrying a shoulder and knee injury that Liz was unaware of, but even without that I'm not very flexible. To give an example, there were three of us in a class and Liz told us to stretch our arms up to the sky and then while keeping them outstretched to swing them slowly forward and down until we were touching our toes. She then looked at me and asked if I had a question. I said, "No. This is just the limit of how far down I can move my arms." Okay, that didn't happen but you get the idea – I'm not flexible. But with the tailored positions I was able to do most of the poses she prescribed.

Following the yoga, she would go into trance and guide me through a regression. I had been regressed many times before but this was vastly different. With her guidance, my first regression was to a past life to see an issue I still had to deal with. During the regression I was guided to heal it. Then we moved from the physical to the spirit world. Okay, that was new for me. I'd never gone to this state in a regression. In the spirit world my life was reviewed and again we healed what came up.

From that point on nearly all my regressions began at a point between lives. I found myself in a huge temple, one I had seen in my dreams a year before. Every time I went back to the temple it had more detail. I realized the temple was a part of me and each regression unlocked more of this place. Soon I could see the vaulted ceiling and was guided up through the window at the top into a blue liquid light that I merged with. Many of my regressions now started in this liquid light.

I was shown how I planned one particular lifetime. From within the liquid, I created a conference room. It looked misshapen when viewing it from the liquid state, but when I transferred my consciousness into the room it appeared perfectly formed. In the room, I occupied what felt like a physical body. I sat at the conference table, looking into a device that showed a projection of my new body, and planned each interaction in the upcoming life. I could move through my planned life using the device, and when I'd come to an important point, I'd pause and examine how I looked and how the person I needed to interact with looked, and review what we needed to cover together. I could adjust how I appeared based on the reaction I wanted to get from the other person. I realized I had extreme control over how I would look in the upcoming lifetime and that it was very important. I could also see who I would meet and what they looked like. For instance, one influential encounter was to be with a homeless man and his appearance was also designed to evoke a reaction from me. Great care was taken by both parties in this planning phase to ensure the encounter went as needed.

While I was planning this life, I could move from the conference room and back into the liquid state as much as I wanted. However, the closer it came to my incarnation the longer I stayed in the room. While in the room I was not the man I would become. I appeared as someone I had already been. The man I would become was only seen through the device on the table, and in my regression I only saw that in black and white. It felt like a system previously created for my physical projection in a former life was being reused for me in the room, and that I could have chosen any former life avatar I wanted.

My regression then moved forward in time and I was that man on the earth plane in San Francisco. Everything was full color now. In that lifetime I was fully aware of my spiritual nature and I was testing something new to me. While I was aware, others were not. I was a young hotel owner and I relished the clientele that came through my door, especially the ones who had travelled far. Everyone had a story. I loved talking to the guests and hearing about their lives and specifically how their philosophies had changed over the course of their lives. I knew them before they incarnated and I was excited about how the planning and the experience shaped the soul within the body. It just worked so well. I even met the homeless man. That was a big one for me. Again, I was aware, but he was not. His philosophy had indeed been reshaped, as planned, based on his life experience.

I Was an Author

In another regression I travelled the seas from England in search of wonders. Everywhere I went, natives were fascinated with us and our advanced technology. I hoped to find a place that was more advanced than us, so I could experience the wonder others felt when we sailed to their lands. I never did. I turned my despair around and decided to write stories of travel that matched my imagination.

I was regressed to a point in that lifetime just before death. I was seated just to the side of a long grand table. Two huge candles illuminated the table from one side. I had to look from the corner of my eye to see the guests. They were the characters I had created in my adventures. We were celebrating. They celebrated me giving them expression and I celebrated the rewards their life had given me in return. The flickering candles added a dimension to the room that aided imagination. The candles flickered around the table to draw attention. Wherever the candle light danced, I witnessed conversation or a raised glass.

My Abilities Are Restored

At the end of many of the regressions I received a healing and a new energy. Each energy was connected with a different ability, such as spiritual healing, connecting with guides, teaching, counseling or compassion. I could see the energies entering my body and interestingly could also feel them. I assume feeling them was due to the work I had previously done feeling energy, but it enhanced my experience.

I had received four energies at one point and each new energy lined up beside the previous one – all in my chest. The next one, however, left a gap and that puzzled me. Near the end of the three days I saw that it wasn't a gap. It was the liquid blue light I kept returning to. I was just not able to see it until my heart had opened more.

Twin Soul

During my regressions, I met several spiritual beings that were very important in my life. Some were quite surprising but one stood out. A few months prior to this trip I had two dreams that really caught my attention. In both dreams a bird came from the heavens down to the earth plane. It definitely predicted a merging with a spirit being, and I interpreted it at the time as me possibly connecting with my higher self.

This spirit being identified herself in one of my early regressions as my twin soul. She gave the name Sofeea. I had heard about soul mates but apparently this is different. We each have a twin soul and both incarnate separately over many lifetimes with the intention of balancing male and female energies and restoring awareness. The intention is that twins reunite when both are enlightened and ascend together.

If there are lots of things that puzzle you in that last paragraph, I'm right there with you. I never cared for stories of ascension or for stories of soul mates. I had never even heard about twin souls until now. However, I do understand dreams and I knew something was coming and she fit the bill.

During one regression a ceremony was held to reunite Sofeea and me. She was ecstatic. So much so that I felt I didn't really get the significance of this. However, I can feel her presence at all times now and it is stronger than how I feel my guides. That is saying a lot because nothing has ever come in stronger than them. She feels like pure love, like the warmest hug you can imagine – a hug from someone that's known and loved you for a very long time. There are never any words. It is purely an emotional embrace. If I tune into it for any length of time I feel so loved that tears come to my eyes. She is working with me to keep my heart chakra open and to help me in my relationship with Sandy.

Lesson learned: You don't always have to understand what's going on. Accept it when you know it is good for you and trust your guides always have your best interest at heart.

The World Is Changing

During trance channeling, Liz shared the same message as Pearson back in 1992. She talked about the world changing and how it is now more important than ever for each of us to connect with our soul, find the spark within, and fan it into a flame. This phase of the earth experiment is drawing to a close.

In a regression, I was shown images of when the human phase started. It was a huge collaboration from within the spirit world. The earth had gone through a long healing process to restore harmony since the previous hominoid experiment. The big question was, "Is this the optimum point to reintroduce hominoids to the planet?" Choosing the right starting point would allow the experiment to run for an optimum duration, as the earth could better sustain itself in the face of the damage hominoids bring. Other factors taken into consideration included how hominoids could sustain themselves, and the diversity and number of opportunities available for growth. There was a balance between the effort required to survive and potential for growth in that lifetime. The human phase was planned at its very beginning to last as long as it has.

I left my vision of the past and was then shown images of potential futures for mankind. Each was very different from today. Each future was heavily influenced by the spirit world. Each future required work on healing the planet from the damage caused by humans. In all potential futures, humans would be aware that the planet belonged to the spirit world.

Inflicting (my word!) dramatic change felt very callous to me and I expressed that feeling. In response, Liz channeled that the density of the earth plane has the potential to liberate but also to ensnare. Many souls repeat lifetimes holding onto negative patterns and remain unaware of their divine spark. Some, through their own actions, regress and lose awareness. This phase has lasted nearly 300,000 years. That is more than long enough to restore awareness, but some souls have not tried at all or not tried hard enough. The experiment was always planned to change and will change. There is still enough time for individuals on the earth plane to reach awareness. Anyone here can still have another lifetime before the change is fully realized.

Although I argued with her, I couldn't deny that her message of change echoed what Pearson had said. I also couldn't help but think of the crystals he had restored in preparation for the spirit world reactivating the Stone Age structures. Through dream analysis, I had also met two people who are here as part of a group to turn that switch. More recently I have met people who are advanced spirits who have incarnated with the express purpose of helping people adjust to the change. There is also solace in the fact that there are souls here on the planet with the express purpose of helping others awaken.

Lesson learned: The world is changing and it is now more important than ever for people to live their life purpose and grasp the opportunities for growth that are presented to them.

I Tune in to My Path

I received a lesson on how to tune in to my path. I saw Seattle and was shown how to see spiritual light in the landscape. The light showed itself as candles illuminating the path for me. Simply focusing caused the edges of the road to become semi-transparent and reveal the illuminated candles. Wherever I stood, the candles created a temple that resembled the great altar from my regressions and spread outward from it. I tried to see my path but it only went about thirty feet before I could no longer see the candles. I got the impression that there was no need to look beyond the present. The candles would only illuminate what was needed in the present. Then I noticed the candles swept a path that ran all the way up the Space Needle. That made sense, I was getting married in five days at the Space Needle. When I focused from that perspective I could see that the candles led somewhere else from the Space Needle, but again they only ran for thirty feet. I got the message. Focus on getting married. Then focus on the next step and only one step at a time. Anything else is a dilution of energy.

The Sword of Light

When I thought we were done, Liz went into trance again and guided me through receiving another energy. While receiving the energy I could see a past life in my mind. What I received was a sword of light that features in Irish mythology. Supposedly, the bearer cannot be harmed in battle. I got the sword and I also saw how to use it from my previous lifetime. It wasn't used how I expected. I had always imagined the bearer wielding it like a regular sword and cutting down their foes with it. Instead the bearer holds the sword in front of them but pointing up to the heavens. It creates a pathway that allows a great light to travel down from the heavens that fills out all around the bearer. It is this light that gives the protection. In my vision the bearer was on a horse and could travel at full speed without fear of attack.

Returning Home

My experience was amazing and the messages were in stark contrast to the first readings I ever received. I put it down to the fact that I had done a lot of work on myself in the meantime.

Heading home I felt like a lot of time had passed with Liz, but at the same time I felt younger. A weight had been lifted from me. It had taken Liz a while to get me to release by crying during the regressions. Now, sitting alone on the plane thinking of Sandy and getting married, I found tears came easily. I was happier than I had been in a very long time and had a new appreciation for people in my life. I wanted to hug everyone! I knew this feeling. I was back on the Dharmic path!

20. Conclusion

A few days after returning from Canada, Sandy and I got married. The ceremony and reception were at the Space Needle. That was as far as I could see in my visions in Canada. A whole five days into the future! If it hadn't been explained to me so well, I would have thought my guides were looking into the wrong end of a telescope. No! The emphasis was to focus on the present so that's what I'm doing.

I still suck at marketing but my guides say I will receive help with promotion. They even named the person so I know who it is. I just can't say her name in case I scare her off!

Finishing this book is a necessary step on my path. It's been fun to write and put into order. Originally it felt egotistical to write about myself but I get it now. Writing this book is for me to acknowledge who I am. It has been a journey with ups and downs, but looking back I can see my own hand in many of the downs and I can see my guides' involvement in keeping me on track.

There are other events and people in my life, whom I have not included in this book, that have pushed me along when I was reluctant or going slowly. I'm lucky that there are far too many to mention. My brother, John, has been invaluable in directly assisting me throughout my life. A boss in Ireland helped enormously by pushing me to learn skills that are vital to me today. Two friends in Seattle dragged me forward by getting me to run courses I originally didn't want to do, taking me out of my comfort zone and forcing me to continue learning. Others made and still make my journey easier with their constant support and love. These are easy to spot. My sister, Pat, played many roles – spiritual companion, adviser, book editor – not happy until it's right! (Psst! Is it okay now, Pat?) Then there's Sandy. Always happy! Always supportive! Always wanting to have fun! A terrible person to be around if you had decided to be depressed.

I'm in the fortunate position that most people share their dreams with me. From their dreams I know that some of these people are guides. But whether a guide or not, many people are agents for progress in my life. Sometimes I don't see it until I look back. I also accept that sometimes I never see it.

Lessons learned: Many people are agents for progress in your life. Karma is subtle. The person who lets you down at just the right time could be fulfilling a promise made before you were born, causing you to see something you would have missed otherwise. Be thankful.

Thank you for reading my story. I hope you get some value from me sharing the lessons I learned.

About The Author

Michael Sheridan

I was born in Dublin, Ireland in 1965. I lived in Alaska in my early twenties and returned to Ireland where I studied psychology at Dublin City University, and studied Dream Interpretation under the veteran, George Rhatigan.

My decades of work and exploration in the spiritual field are as a result of a spontaneous awakening I experienced at age 27, and the ripples I've experienced ever since. I've been interviewed countless times on National TV and radio because of my expertise in dreams. I moved to Seattle in 2011 and currently host the radio show, "So, You Think You're Awake?" on KKNW.

I live with my wife, Sandy, two daughters, Heidi and Julie, and two grandsons, Billie (4) and Thomas (2). Billie and Thomas sometimes allow me to relax and watch TV very late in the evening. I work, write, and prepare for my radio show from home. Life is good!

Email: michael@dream-analysis.com URL: www.dream-analysis.com

How To Interpret Your Dreams *and discover your life purpose*

I'm very proud of this book, written in 2007. It contains detailed lessons on each topic that I cover on my dream courses. It also includes sections on psychic development and a comprehensive dream symbol dictionary (compiled from the analysis of real dreams).

Amazon URL: `amzn.to/1JKInhG`

Dream Interpretation Courses

I run courses, mostly in Seattle, where I share my passion for spiritual development. I love to help people discover their gifts and unlock how their gifts are best used. My courses rely heavily on dreams because they are like an open letter for me. They are a lifeline from your higher-self that gives detailed direction on all aspects of your life. Your higher-self needs you to grow spiritually, to increase your awareness. To do that you need to remain on your path and stay true to your purpose. Many dreams remind you of that path and recommend adjustments to help you stay true to it. Depending on how true you've been some adjustments may be severe. The more severe they are, the more important it is to make them.

Your higher self also wants (needs) you to be healthy, so many dreams comment directly on how to remain healthy or how to restore your health. This is vital and valuable information that sadly goes unheeded by most people.

Topics covered on my Dream Interpretation course are usually in the following order. Courses are run with a good sense of humor!

1. The four rules of interpretation
2. Objectivity with the *I AM* and *I NEED* formula
3. Health Dreams: The Digestive & Elimination System
4. The spiritual dimension of dreams
5. How to recognize spiritual dreams
6. Spiritual Abilities: Counselling
7. Spiritual Abilities: Intuition
8. Health Dreams: The Circulatory System & Emotional Health
9. Spiritual Abilities: Hands-on Healing
10. Mind and body
11. Spiritual Abilities: Hypnosis & Projection
12. Spiritual Abilities: Communication with Spirits
13. Your dreams interpreted
14. Health Dreams: The Reproductive System
15. Life purpose dreams
16. Therapies for dealing with issues raised in dreams
17. Health Dreams: The Respiratory System
18. Numbers in dreams
19. Colors in dreams
20. Spiritual Abilities: Spiritual Teacher & Leader
21. Spiritual Abilities: Writer
22. Spiritual Abilities: Prophetic
23. How to see auras
24. How to see spirit guides

Optional (depending on time)

1. Clearing your aura
2. Feeling the aura
3. Feeling the presence of your guides
4. Using a Pendulum to Help with Analysis

URL: www.dream-analysis.com/workshop

Combination Channeling & Dream Courses

These courses are run in tandem with Heidi Brooke. In addition to the list above, Heidi's modules include the following

1. Protections
2. How to ground yourself
3. Using a pendulum
4. Establishing connection with your Guides
5. Recognizing (feeling) your Guides and Guardian Angels
6. Welcoming communication from passed on loved ones
7. The differences in how spirits of different levels communicate
8. Clearing and removing negative influences/entities
9. Putting/pointing you on your path
10. Seeing spirits and auras
11. Raising your vibration to meditate
12. Opening your chakras
13. Color-breath healing, are you a healer?
14. Recognizing your intuition and using it [and our inherent ability to mind read/body read]
15. Addressing individual diet to maintain health and connection

URL: www.dream-analysis.com/workshop

Online Courses

I'm currently changing my online courses to make them more accessible. To that end I'm recording a series of videos that cover the knowledge aspects. My intention is to grant lifetime access to course participants (for both online or in-person courses) so they can be viewed at leisure or when a dream broaches a topic.

URL: www.dream-analysis.com/online

Radio Show – So, You Think You're Awake?

This is my radio show with Susan Pullen (left) and Heidi Brooke (right). It's a weekly one-hour show detailing how your dreams from last night attempt to awaken you to the important issues in your life today. Dream topics include relationships, career, life purpose, health, spiritual abilities and more. In this live call-in, I smash the myths and demonstrate the art of Dream Interpretation by telling you exactly what your dreams mean.

Tune into the show on Thursdays at Noon on 1150 (AM Dial) KKNW

URL: www.dream-analysis.com/kknw.htm

Made in the USA
Middletown, DE
02 April 2021